THE HIGHEST STAGE
OF CAPITALISM

IMPERIALISM, THE HIGHEST STAGE OF CAPITALISM

A Popular Outline

V.I. Lenin

Introduction by Prabhat Patnaik

Imperialism, the Highest Stage of Capitalism was written by Lenin between January and June 1916.
First published mid-1917 in pamphlet form by Zhizn i. Znaniye Publishers, Petrograd.
'Preface to the French and German Editions' first published in *Communist International*, No. 18, 1921.
This translation is taken from volume 1 of Lenin's three-volume *Selected Works* (Moscow: Progress Publishers, 1977).

This edition first published January 2000
Reprinted September 2010
by LeftWord Books
12 Rajendra Prasad Road
New Delhi 110 001
India
Web: www.leftword.com
Email: leftword@gmail.com

LeftWord Books is a division of
Naya Rasta Publishers Pvt. Ltd.

Introduction by Prabhat Patnaik © 2000, LeftWord Books

ISBN   978-81-87496-07-6

Printed at Progressive Printers
A 21 Jhilmil Industrial Area
Grand Trunk Road
Shahdara
Delhi 110 095
India

CONTENTS

CONTENTS

INTRODUCTION

Prabhat Patnaik

Lenin's *Imperialism* is one of the most significant books of the twentieth century. Its significance arises not so much from the details or the data it provides; nor does it arise from the sheer fact that it 'explains' imperialism and the World War. The book is significant because it provides the steel-frame for a grand reconstruction of Marxism (within which the 'explanation' for wars is located) which becomes the basis for revolutionary praxis for the rest of the twentieth century.

It is therefore a very unusual book. Lenin did not just happen to develop a theory (of imperialism) and put it down on paper, as is usually the case with other authors and books. Rather, he saw the need for a grand reconstruction of Marxism and the outline of what such a structure should look like, and then set out to erect the steel-frame for it. The inspiration for the book in other words comes from the crisis of praxis that had engulfed the working class movement upon the outbreak of the First World War, rather than from some sudden blinding 'illumination' regarding the nature of imperialism *per se*. Lenin saw the theoretical void whose filling was essential for revolutionary praxis, and filled it with a work which made use of whatever data happened to be available. The profundity of this work would not have changed an iota if he had put in twice as much data, or half as much.

Paradoxically, however, for this very reason, *Imperialism* is one of Lenin's less appreciated works. Much of the book is filled with information which does not make easy reading; and it is information relating to a period long past, culled from authors long forgotten. At the same time the theoretical significance of the work is not easily apparent since the void it fills is not visible, precisely because it has been filled. The book has the quality of deceiving the reader into missing its profundity.

To appreciate the significance of *Imperialism* it is necessary therefore to recapture the historical conjuncture in which it was written and which gave rise to the theoretical confusion (or what I have called 'theoretical void') underlying the crisis of praxis.

I

Almost at the very moment when Marxism succeeded in establishing its theoretical sway over the European, and in particular the German working class movement, it was confronted with an altogether new challenge. This challenge came not from the followers of Bakunin, or of Proudhon, or of Lassalle, but from within its own ranks. Eduard Bernstein, a friend of Engels since 1888 and a prominent member of the German Social Democratic Party, argued in 1901 for an extensive 'revision' of Marxism (which is the origin of the term 'revisionism'). The Marxist perception of the need for a revolutionary overthrow of capitalism, he argued, derived from the view that it was a historically doomed system, that it was moving towards an economic breakdown anyway. But since such a breakdown had neither occurred nor was anywhere in sight, the agenda for the revolutionary overthrow of the system should be shelved in favour of struggles within the system for the economic betterment of the working class. The proletariat, in other words, should give up its revolutionary socialist programme, and settle down to peaceful trade unionism within the system. What is more, since the 'will of the majority' prevails in a democracy, the introduction of political freedom, democracy, and universal suffrage in bourgeois society removes the basis for believing any longer that the state is an organ of class-rule. Bernstein's position was summed up by his remark: 'The movement is everything, the ultimate aim is nothing'. To remain occupied exclusively with the empirical day-to-day activity of trade unionism and petty politics with the aim of gaining advantages of the moment, and to forget about the basic features of the whole capitalist system, about the direction of its evolution, and about the primary goal of bringing in socialism: such was Bernstein's advice to the working class.

Bernstein was not alone in suggesting a 'revisionist' programme; and the programme too was comprehensive, not confined only to the sphere of economic and political activity, but encompassing the realm of theory as well, both philosophy and political economy. Indeed, Lenin saw the comprehensiveness and the pervasiveness of revisionism as a positive development reflecting an objective trend towards the overcoming of heterogeneity.

Even though the revisionist tendency was sharply attacked within each Social Democratic Party, it made deep inroads into the working class movement. When the First World War intervened, the extent of the sway of revisionism, which found expression in the form of 'social patriotism' and 'social chauvinism', became apparent. Within most European Social Democratic Parties (Russia being the only major exception) the majority of the leadership lined up behind 'its national' war effort; Social Democratic deputies voted everywhere for war credits in their respective Parliaments. And when the President of the Second International, the Belgian Socialist Vandervelde was requested in 1915 to convene a session of the Executive of the International to discuss the situation, so that the European working class movement could take some common position on the war, his reply was typically social-chauvinist: 'As long as German soldiers are billeted in the homes of Belgian workers, there can be no talk of convening the Executive'![1]

The rot that had set in was best illustrated by Germany. The German Social Democratic Party had struck deep roots in the working class and had emerged as the largest single socialist force in the whole of Europe. It had a galaxy of leaders that included Karl Kautsky who had acquired great stature owing to his command over the Marxist texts, his friendship with Engels, and his struggle against Bernstein's revisionism. The strength and reach of the German Social Democratic Party can be gauged from the fact that on the eve of the First World War, it brought out as many as 86 daily newspapers in Germany!

---

[1] Isaac Deutscher, *The Prophet Armed*, Oxford: OUP, 1954, p. 225.

And yet when the War broke out, instead of taking a forthright stand in opposition to the War, the majority of the leadership of the German Social Democratic Party took an opportunist position. When war credits were being voted in the German Reichstag in 1914, all the Social Democratic Deputies (of whom there were 110), with the exception of Karl Liebknecht and Otto Ruhle, voted in favour. Karl Liebknecht, who had already been sentenced for 'high treason' in 1907 for his book *Militarism and Anti-Militarism,* and had written another important pamphlet entitled *The Main Enemy is Within the Country,* belonged, together with Franz Mehring, Clara Zetkin, Leo Jogiches and Rosa Luxemburg, to a small minority within the leadership of the German Social Democratic Party which took a forthright position against social chauvinism.

Three distinct positions emerged within European Social Democracy on the question of war. There was first of all the straightforward social-chauvinist position, which was held by the majority of the leadership in most Parties.[2] Secondly, there was a 'Centrist' position held by Kautsky, Longuet, Turati, Ramsay Macdonald and Martov among others, which, while opposing social-chauvinism, did not wish to break with the social-chauvinist elements within Social Democracy, and, while opposing the War, wanted to fight for peace rather than revolution. In Lenin's words,

> The 'Centre' all vow and declare that they are Marxists and internationalists, that they are for peace, for bringing every kind of 'pressure' to bear upon the governments, for 'demanding' in every way that their own government should 'ascertain the will of the people for peace', that they are for all sorts of peace campaigns, for peace without annexations, etc. etc.– *and for peace with the social-chauvinists.* The 'Centre' is for unity, the Centre is opposed to a split.[3]

The third position, held by Lenin, Liebknecht, Luxemburg, Radek and others, was summed up by the title of Liebknecht's pamphlet *The Main Enemy is Within the Country.* It believed that 'the problem of war

---

[2] Its adherents within Russia included such stalwarts as Plekhanov, Zasulich and Potressov.

[3] *Collected Works,* Moscow: Progress Publishers, volume 24, p. 76.

can be solved only in a revolutionary way', that since it was an imperialist war for a division of the 'spoils', to talk of a war against war is meaningless unless it is directed against 'one's own' imperialist bourgeoisie. The proletariat therefore should convert the imperialist war into a revolutionary civil war to overthrow the imperialist bourgeoisie. This third position wanted a complete break from social-chauvinism, and hence from 'Centrism' (since the latter was unwilling to break from social-chauvinism), and the setting up of a new International of revolutionary Marxists.

While the official Second International rejected any meeting of European workers' representatives to discuss the situation arising out of the War, an International Socialist Conference was nevertheless organized at the initiative of the Italian Socialists at Zimmerwald (a small Swiss village close to Berne) in September 1915, which brought together 38 delegates from 11 countries, including, significantly, from countries which were at war with one another.[4] A resolution moved by Lenin calling for a civil war and the setting up of a new International was defeated by 19 votes to 12. The minority around Lenin, the 'Zimmerwald Left', however supported, despite recording its reservations, the main resolution which condemned the War (without however specifying any alternative course of action). The Zimmerwald Left emerged as the rallying point for all internationalist forces at a second conference at Kienthal in 1916,[5] and became the forerunner of the Communist International.

The positions articulated in *Imperialism* therefore had already been a part of the understanding and the programme which Lenin, as the leader of the authentic internationalist section of the Socialist movement, had been advocating for some time. However, while putting together in a single comprehensive document positions which were already being aired for some time, *Imperialism* gave these positions theoretical roots, by locating them within the corpus of Marxist political economy.

The difference between the character of Luxemburg's and Lenin's books on imperialism (without going into the contents of the two books) is quite marked in this respect: Lenin's book is overwhelmingly, insistently, passionately concerned with praxis, while Luxemburg's is an incisive tract

---

[4] The countries represented were France, Germany, Russia, Italy, Poland, Romania, Bulgaria, Switzerland, The Netherlands, Norway and Sweden.

[5] It functioned with a coordinating committee consisting of Lenin, Zinoviev and Radek.

on abstract theory. But as Lukács once remarked: 'The highest level of development of theory is when theory bursts into praxis.'[6] Lenin's *Imperialism* is indeed theory bursting into praxis.

II

While the crisis of praxis facing the European workers' movement in the context of the War might have been the immediate provocation behind *Imperialism*, the theory advanced in the book did much more than merely provide a solution to this crisis. Indeed the hallmark of *Imperialism* lies in the fact that while providing a theoretical answer to the problem of praxis of the European working class movement, it widened the scope of revolutionary praxis itself to cover the oppressed nations as well. The theory it put forward permitted the linking up of the two main currents of revolutionary struggle in the twentieth century. The International it helped to found was an International the like of which had not been seen till then. It was an International in the true sense of the term, where delegates from India, China and Vietnam would hobnob with those from Germany, Britain and France.

Even though Marx and Engels had been preoccupied with the proletarian revolution in Europe, the question of revolution in the colonies had made fleeting appearances in several of their letters and journalistic writings. Marx in his 8 August 1853 article in the *New York Daily Tribune* had written: 'The Indians will not reap the fruits of the new elements of society scattered among them by the British bourgeoisie till in Great Britain itself the now ruling classes shall have been supplanted by the industrial proletariat, or till the Hindoos themselves shall have grown strong enough to throw off the English yoke altogether.' And Engels in a letter to Kautsky on 12 September 1882 had written: 'India will perhaps, indeed very probably, produce a revolution. . . . The same thing might also take place elsewhere, e.g. in Algiers and Egypt, and would certainly be the best thing *for us.*'

Lenin not only brought this subterranean stream of thinking into the open, he not only placed the question of revolution in the East as much on the agenda as the revolution in the imperialist countries, but,

[6] G. Lukács, *Lenin*, London: NLB, 1970.

what is more, *he made the revolution in the East as much a business of the Communist International as that in the imperialist countries.* It is in this respect that he broke completely new ground. And the theoretical expression of this perception that the two revolutions were dialectically related, that one could not talk of the one without being concerned about the other, was contained in *Imperialism.* In the preface to the French and German editions of *Imperialism*, Lenin himself clarified this composite picture of dual oppression in the following words:

> But as a matter of fact the capitalist threads, which in thousands of different intercrossings bind these enterprises with private property in the means of production in general, have converted this railway construction into an instrument for oppressing *a thousand million* people (in the colonies and semi-colonies), that is, more than half the population of the globe that inhabits the dependent countries, as well as the wage-slaves of capital in the 'civilized' countries.

The fact that these '*thousand million*' people are now brought to the centre-stage of revolutionary theory on a par with the wage-slaves of 'civilized' countries, which, till then had been the exclusive focus of attention, is a fact of momentous significance.

Seeing the revolutionary potential of these 'thousand million' people was not just pious hope or wishful thinking. It was a reading of what was actually happening. Lenin had noted that '1905 was followed by revolutions in Turkey, Persia and China, and that a revolutionary movement developed in India'.[7] He had commented on the fact that the arrest of Tilak had been followed by a General Strike of workers in Bombay. He had also noted both the enormous leap in the consciousness of the colonial people and the growth in their capacity to use arms ('a very useful thing') which had come about as a result of their employment as canon-fodder in the imperialist war. Lenin, in other words, saw the revolutionary process in the colonies and dependencies actually acquiring much greater vigour in the pre-War and War years.

Soon he would place even greater reliance on the struggle of the

---

[7] *Selected Works*, Moscow: Progress Publishers, 1975, volume 3, p. 246.

oppressed peoples than he had done in *Imperialism*. As the prospects of a European, especially German, revolution receded, Lenin increasingly pinned his hopes on the revolutionary struggles in the East. 'In the last analysis', he wrote in 1923,

> the outcome of the struggle will be determined by the fact that Russia, India, China, etc., account for the overwhelming majority of the population of the globe. And during the last few years it is this majority that has been drawn into the struggle for emancipation with extraordinary rapidity, so that in this respect there cannot be the slightest doubt what the final outcome of the world struggle will be. In this sense the complete victory of socialism is fully and absolutely assured.[8]

This understanding, however, was to come later. *Imperialism* still hoped for an imminent revolution that could break out *anywhere*. The immediate hurdles were supposed to be the 'corrupt' social-chauvinist leaders and their 'spineless' social-pacifist camp-followers, from whose influence the proletariat had to be emancipated.

III

In the process of carrying out this basic reconstruction of Marxism, Lenin provided answers to a number of other vexing questions. Indeed there are at least five other fundamental issues on which the unified conception developed by Lenin and expounded in *Imperialism* brought clarity of understanding.

First, it provided a novel answer to a crucial question left unanswered by Marx, who had said: 'No social order ever perishes before all the productive forces for which there is room in it have developed'.[9] The question left unanswered was: are there any objective criteria on the basis of which one can say that a social order has reached its historical limit? Marx's remark in *The Poverty of Philosophy* that 'of all the instruments of production, the greatest productive power is the revolutionary class

---

[8] Ibid., p. 725.
[9] Preface to *A Contribution to the Critique of Political Economy*, Marx and Engels, *Selected Works*, London: Lawrence and Wishart, 1970, p. 182.

itself',[10] might suggest that the formation of the revolutionary class itself constitutes the limit of a mode of production: there are no other independent objective criteria to determine when a mode of production passes over from being historically progressive to being historically moribund and reactionary. But such a view appears voluntaristic, contrary to the materialist standpoint.

Eduard Bernstein, as we have seen, had interpreted the exhaustion of capitalism's historical potential as being synonymous with an economic breakdown of the system. Those like Rosa Luxemburg who held aloft the revolutionary banner within German Social Democracy against Bernstein's revisionism, adopted ironically the same interpretation as Bernstein, but proceeded to show that capitalism was indeed headed for a collapse. In short, the identification of a collapse with the limit of the system became common both to the revisionist and the revolutionary wings of Social Democracy. (Lenin himself had this position in 1908.)[11] The former denied and the latter asserted its inevitability.

Lenin's *Imperialism* however produced an altogether different perspective which was less scholastic and more practical. Imperialism produces wars. It forces workers from one country to kill fellow workers from another, across trenches. The only way the workers can avoid this is by turning their guns against their masters. Imperialism in other words offers the workers only one choice: to destroy themselves and their fellow workers, or to overthrow the capitalist system (hence the Bolshevik slogan: 'convert the imperialist war into a civil war'). Since it poses this final choice, between revolution or social destruction, imperialism *is* the limit of capitalism. When capitalism enters its monopoly stage (which Lenin took to be identical with imperialism), it has already exhausted its potential, it has become moribund. A practical *denouement* based on Marx's own theory (which explained the emergence of monopoly through centralization of capital) was thus provided to the historical process outlined by Marx, completing the conceptual characterization of that process.

Secondly, Lenin not only linked the two most powerful revolutionary streams of this century, the proletarian revolutionary struggles of

---

[10] Marx and Engels, *Collected Works*, New York: International Publishers, volume 6, p. 211.

[11] 'Marxism and Revisionism', *Selected Works*, Moscow: Progress Publishers, 1977, volume 1, p. 53.

the advanced capitalist countries and the struggle for national liberation in the colonies; he not only made the latter struggle too a matter of intervention by the proletariat and hence of concern to the International; but he also gave a definite shape to the strategy to be followed in this struggle. He insisted of course on a concrete analysis of the situation in each country and a differentiated set of tactics to be pursued across countries depending on the concrete conditions. But he set out the overall perspective on this question at the Second Congress of the Communist International.

This perspective *inter alia* had two important components. First, the Communist International and the Communist Parties must support the 'bourgeois-democratic liberation movement' in the colonial and backward countries, but only on the condition that the independence of the proletarian movement, 'even if it is in its most embryonic form', is upheld under all circumstances. Secondly, special support must be given to the peasant movement 'against the landowners, against landed proprietorship, and against all manifestations and survivals of feudalism', and every effort should be exerted to 'apply the basic principle of the Soviet system in countries where pre-capitalist relations predominate – by setting up "working people's Soviets," etc.'[12]

At the Second Congress, as is well-known, M.N. Roy objected to Lenin's thesis on supporting 'bourgeois-democratic' national movements on the grounds that 'a certain *rapprochement* had developed between the bourgeoisie of the exploiting countries and that of the colonies, so that very often the bourgeoisie of the oppressed countries, while it does support the national movement, is in full accord with the imperialist bourgeoisie, i.e., joins forces with it against all revolutionary movements and revolutionary classes'.[13] As a result, the final report which was adopted unanimously represented a compromise where the term 'bourgeois-democratic' was replaced by the term 'national-revolutionary'.

This compromise, it has been argued, had 'the effect of blunting the sharp edge of Lenin's thought and of bridging disagreement by resort to a potential ambiguity.'[14] In any case the question of the Communist

---

[12] *Selected Works*, volume 3, p. 376.

[13] This is the way Lenin summed up the criticism against his position; see *Selected Works*, volume 3, p. 406.

[14] E.H. Carr, *The Bolshevik Revolution: 1917–1923*, Harmondsworth, 1966, volume 3, p. 256.

movement's attitude to the bourgeoisie in the colonial and dependent countries was to become a vexed question which occupied the Communist International for long, and on which the International's position went through several twists and turns (during the Sixth and the Seventh Congresses). What is more, all the issues of the Second Congress debate, namely the attitude to adopt towards the bourgeoisie, the possibility of by-passing the capitalist phase of development in newly-liberated countries, were to emerge once again in a new incarnation after decolonization. Indeed, they are still with us. While the debate everywhere at the current moment is not necessarily on identical issues, nonetheless some subset or the other of these issues, in various refracted forms, is being debated not only in countries which have adopted the capitalist path of development after national liberation, but even in countries which were in a position to embark on the socialist path.

The remarkable thing however, is that in essence these issues had been posed by Lenin as early as 1920. This was possible because he sought to see concretely, for defining correct praxis, the relationship between the two revolutionary streams, which he saw imperialism and the imperialist War as having necessarily linked. The War, he argued, not only offers the workers the ultimate choice between revolution and mutual destruction, but also draws 'dependent peoples' into world history, and helps the revolution in these countries too.

Imperialism, then, is the eve of social revolution. This revolution is not confined to any particular part of the globe, but takes on the character of a world revolution. The use of the concept of a 'general crisis of capitalism' which appeared in the programme of the International, was the theoretical expression of this understanding.

Thirdly, this theoretical understanding also had to explain exceptions to itself. Why was it that when world revolution had come on the agenda, some of the greatest luminaries of social democracy, not to mention significant sections of the working class in the advanced capitalist countries, were taking revisionist, and even downright social-chauvinist, positions? Lenin's theory of imperialism provided a novel answer to this.

Lenin had already attempted once before to explain revisionism. His explanation had been as follows: 'A number of new "middle strata" are inevitably brought into existence again and again by capitalism. These small producers are just as inevitably being cast again into the ranks of the proletariat. It is quite natural that the petty-bourgeois world outlook should again and again crop up in the ranks of the broad workers' parties.'[15]

This explanation, offered in 1908, would have certainly appeared inadequate after the outbreak of the War. In *Imperialism* therefore Lenin provided an altogether different explanation for the phenomenon, namely the fact that monopoly super-profits were used in the imperialist countries to bribe a 'thin upper stratum' of the working class, the 'workers' aristocracy', and certain trade unionists and leaders of the workers' movement. Lenin's theoretical inspiration for this position came from certain remarks that Engels had made in two of his letters. And Lenin's own position, in turn, has been the springboard for a vast literature on 'unequal exchange' that has developed since his time to explain the dwindling revolutionary influence within the working class in the advanced capitalist countries.

The theory of 'unequal exchange', as it has developed in the writings of Emmanuel, Amin and others, has attracted much controversy; but both sides in the controversy in my view have taken theoretically untenable positions.[16] The entire discussion of unequal exchange is set in a world where wage differences exist across countries, and are sustained by international immobility of labour, even in conditions which otherwise resemble free competition, i.e., in which there is no collusive price-setting and there is free international mobility of capital. The wage differences for labour that is otherwise homogeneous (after allowing for skill-differences) entail, in such a case, a deviation of relative prices from the prices of production that would prevail if the wage rate and the rate of profit were equalized across all commodities: the commodity produced by the low-wage country has a lower relative price than if prices of production prevailed. Wage differences, in other words, sustain, and are in turn sustained by, unequal exchange in the sense of a deviation of relative prices from the relative prices of production. The entire working class in the high-wage country is therefore the beneficiary of unequal exchange.

The argument put forward by Bettelheim against this position is that the productivity differential across countries is even higher than the wage differential. Relative to their level of productivity, in other words,

---

[15] *Selected Works*, volume 1, p. 55.

[16] Arghiri Emmanuel, *Unequal Exchange: A Study of the Imperialism of Trade*, London: NLB, 1972; Samir Amin, *Unequal Development*, New Delhi, 1979. Charles Bettelheim's criticism of Emmanuel's theory is contained in his Introduction to *Unequal Exchange*.

the workers in the advanced capitalist countries are *less well-paid* than the workers in the backward countries. Far from being beneficiaries of the super-exploitation of backward country workers, they are therefore even *more* exploited than the workers in the backward countries.

Bettelheim's position is obviously untenable, since the *observed* wage-productivity ratio is not an index of exploitation. Under free competition in any capitalist economy where there is free mobility of capital and labour from one activity to another, so that both the wage rate (for given intensity of work and length of working day) and the rate of profit are equalized, there would still be unequal wage-productivity ratios (productivity necessarily being evaluated at the equilibrium prices of production): workers in activities with higher organic composition of capital would have a lower wage-productivity ratio. But this signifies nothing regarding the intensity of exploitation, since the very fact that all workers are paid equal wages for work of the same intensity and spanning the same length of working day implies *ipso facto* identical exploitation.[17] Bettelheim's criterion for judging exploitation therefore is incorrect.

On the other hand the setting in which Emmanuel et al. discuss unequal exchange is itself logically untenable.[18] If Indian workers are paid less than, say, the British workers, and this underlies the fact that commodity A produced by India is under-priced relative to commodity B produced by Britain, then, if capital mobility is being assumed, why don't British capitalists start producing commodity B itself in India? Or, alternatively, why don't Indian capitalists, instead of being inexorably tied to the production of A, start producing B with the cheaper labour available to them, and underselling the British capitalists? The only answer to this

---

[17] The following remark of Marx should clarify his views on the determinants of the degree of exploitation, i.e., of the rate of surplus value: 'And although the equalizing of wages and working days, *and thereby of the rates of surplus value,* among different spheres of production . . . , is checked by all kinds of local obstacles, it is nevertheless taking place more and more with the advance of capitalist production.' *Capital,* volume III, Moscow: Progress Publishers, 1974, p.142.

[18] For a more elaborate discussion of the criticism which follows see the Introduction to *Lenin and Imperialism,* edited by Prabhat Patnaik, Delhi: Orient Longman, 1986. See also the articles by Utsa Patnaik ('Neo-Marxian Theories of Capitalism and Underdevelopment: Towards a Critique'), Krishna Bharadwaj ('A Note on Emmanuel's "Unequal exchange"'), and Usha Menon ('The Concept of Value and Theories of Unequal Exchange') in the same volume.

question can be that there is exercise of monopoly power (by the British capitalists) together with *immobility* of capital (as well as of labour). In other words, unequal exchange can occur plausibly only in the presence of *monopoly*, which is exactly the direction that Lenin's writings point to, but which is totally at variance with the recent theories of unequal exchange.

Fourthly, Lenin's theory of imperialism gave a unity to Lenin's own thoughts, and defined Leninism as a unified totality. There would be general agreement that *What is to be Done?* (1902), *Imperialism* (1916) and *The State and Revolution* (1917) constitute three key documents of Leninism.[19] To these three, however, one should also add Lenin's writings on the agrarian question and the need for the worker–peasant alliance, exemplified by *Two Tactics of Social Democracy in the Democratic Revolution* (1905).[20] If we take these four documents, then, between them, they give a characterization of the epoch, discuss the nature of the bourgeois state in this epoch and hence the meaning of the revolution, describe the class alliance necessary for the revolution in a country like Russia, and explain the nature of the Party structure that is needed for carrying out the revolution. Between them they constitute a more or less complete analysis of the revolutionary process, an analysis, which, even when it is specifically anchored in the Russian situation (as in *Two Tactics*), has profound general implications.

Now, two of these were written before *Imperialism*. In other words, Lenin was in the process of developing the essentials of Leninism as a unified system even before he wrote *Imperialism*. Nonetheless this unity is sealed and everything falls into its place with *Imperialism*. The need to smash the bourgeois state, which, notwithstanding its *form*, is an ossified apparatus of class-repression, emerges with greater clarity, when the state is seen as resting on a 'personal union' between industrial

---

[19] *What is to be Done?* was written in 1902. But even after twenty-four years during which Lenin had written *Imperialism* and *The State and Revolution*, Krupskaya wrote about it that 'it must be studied by everyone who wants to be a Leninist in practice, and not in words alone.' *Memories of Lenin*, London, 1970, p. 61.

[20] The significance of Lenin's writings on this subject can be gauged from the fact that in 1905 itself, Karl Kautsky, then regarded as 'the most consistent and revolutionary pupil of Marx' had written in *Neue Zeit* that the urban revolutionary movement in Russia should remain neutral on the question of the relations between the peasantry and the landowners. See ibid., p.110.

magnates, the financial oligarchy, and the top personnel of the bureaucracy and the army. Likewise the role of the Party as a disciplined band of professional revolutionaries emerges with greater clarity when the need for it to lead the working class in a Clauswitzian struggle against the ossified, oppressive, imperialist state is appreciated. Similarly, the fact that the democratic revolution would have to be led by the proletariat in alliance with the peasantry, and no longer by the bourgeoisie, emerges with greater clarity when it is understood that the bourgeoisie in its monopoly phase makes common cause with all forms of reaction. In short, Lenin's theory of imperialism unifies the different strands of his thinking, giving them a remarkable coherence, even though some of the strands themselves were developed before he wrote *Imperialism*.

Finally, the unity of Lenin's thought, though based on Marx, represented a further development of Marx. This development had necessarily to take selected aspects of Marx's writing as its base. Implicit in this development, in other words, was a distinction drawn, within the totality of Marx's writings, between the 'core' of Marx's thought which could be taken over, and an additional construction around this 'core' which could be substituted. This dichotomy, together with its implication that all Marxist theorizing represents a reconstruction, comes out clearly in *Imperialism*. In unravelling the dynamics of capitalism, Lenin makes no mention for example of the falling tendency of the rate of profit that Marx had talked about; but he makes copious use of J.A. Hobson's writings, even though Hobson himself was intellectually far removed from Marxism. He makes use of Hobson's insights, however, by incorporating them into a Marxist framework, i.e., by building around a Marxist core. In short, *Imperialism* constitutes a practical demonstration of the use of the Marxist method.

Two points stand out from this demonstration: first, as already mentioned, all Marxist theorizing is a reconstruction. Second, the purpose of this reconstruction is to aid praxis. From the proposition (emphasized by Althusser) about the lack of identity between the object of thought and the real object, it follows that the bridge between the two can be provided only by praxis. The test of any reconstruction lies in the validity of the praxis to which it gives rise. *Imperialism* is permeated by this understanding. Indeed its overwhelming concern, as already noted, is with praxis.

Imperialism is also one of Lenin's most misunderstood works as regards its central argument. The reason for this misunderstanding is in my view the following: it is generally taken for granted that a theory of imperialism must be a functional theory. It must have a particular form, where it first shows why capitalism in the absence of imperialism cannot be sustained within the metropolis, and then demonstrates how imperialism specifically rescues capitalism from these insurmountable contradictions. Although Lenin's theory is not of this genre, a theory of this genre has been almost invariably read into Lenin. This has resulted not only in a distortion of his views, but also in the levelling against him of a whole range of illicit criticisms.[21]

The most common such theory read into Lenin is under-consumptionism, and strangely enough no less a person than John Strachey, for long the leading British Communist theoretician, provided such an interpretation of Lenin after abandoning Communism.[22] The under-consumptionist argument runs as follows: the emergence of monopoly capitalism implies a shift of income distribution away from the workers, the non-capitalist petty producers, and the non-monopoly capitalist producers, towards the monopolists. Since the propensity to consume of the monopolists is lower than that of the strata from whom such income distribution shifts occur, these shifts entail a reduction in consumption demand relative to what it would have been under competitive capitalism for an identical level of social output. Other things being equal, this in turn means that the shift to monopoly pushes the economy into an over-production crisis. True, such a crisis would not occur if investment could increase to compensate for the reduction in consumption, but there is no reason why this should happen at all. On the contrary if the economy does face an over-production crisis then its level of investment would get further lowered compared to what it otherwise would have been. In short, the transition from competitive to monopoly capitalism (or any further increase in monopoly profit margins in conditions of monopoly capitalism itself) would, other things remaining

[21] For a somewhat more detailed discussion of the issues of this section see my Introduction to *Lenin and Imperialism*.
[22] John Strachey, *The End of Empire*, London: Gollancz.

the same, push the economy towards generalized over-production.

A specific form of the under-consumption argument which is of some historical relevance is the following: in the transition to monopoly capitalism, the shift in income distribution in favour of the monopolists and away from the petty producers would take the form of an adverse shift in the inter-sectoral terms of trade for the primary producers, since the petty producers, in the guise of the peasantry, are likely to be producing primary commodities for ultimate processing in a manufacturing sector that is typically dominated by the monopolists. The fact that the peasants consume a larger proportion of their income than the monopoly capitalists, would in such a case entail a decline in exports from the manufacturing to the primary commodity sector without an offsetting increase in the internal demand of the manufacturing sector for its own output. This, other things remaining the same, would give rise to a crisis of over-production.

If we focus on the world economy as a whole, then this income shift from the petty producers to the monopoly capitalists would show in terms of a secular shift in the terms of trade against primary producers, and in favour of manufacturing, *as far as international prices are concerned.* The tendency towards over-production in this case would show itself as a sluggishness of exports (other than what is financed by loans and other forms of capital exports) from the metropolitan countries *taken together,* which are the manufacturing centre of the world economy, to the primary commodity-producing Third World countries which suffer terms of trade losses, without a spontaneous offsetting increase in their domestic demand.

Finally, the tendency towards an over-production crisis can also arise for a reason that is altogether different from under-consumption. In the transition from competitive to monopoly capitalism, even if the magnitude of consumption relative to output remains unchanged, the magnitude of investment relative to output is likely to decline. This is because many investment projects which are expected to fetch the average rate of profit in the economy would not be taken up by the monopolists who earn a higher-than-average rate of profit. A shift in income distribution from the non-monopoly to the monopoly capitalists therefore would, other things remaining the same, reduce the level of investment below what it would otherwise have been, and hence give rise to generalized over-production on account of what one might call 'under-investment'.

To say all this does not of course mean that over-production would actually happen. The tendency towards over-production, immanent in the transition from competitive to monopoly capitalism, can be offset by imperialism if it entails an export surplus financed by capital exports. In other words, a logically consistent theory of imperialism can be built up which sees imperialism as functionally necessary for capitalism as it moves into the monopoly phase. Not only is such a theory logically consistent, it is historically plausible as well.

Indeed each of the different lines of argument advanced above can stand the test of historical scrutiny. The secular decline in the terms of trade for the primary producers from the onset of monopoly capitalism until the Second World War has been attested to by a host of writers, starting from Raul Prebisch.[23] The fact that this decline was because of the rise in the 'degree of monopoly' (to use Kalecki's term), i.e., the fact that its coinciding with the era of monopoly capitalism was not an accidental phenomenon, has been argued by several economic historians.[24] The fact that this was a cause of sluggish export growth of Britain (leaving aside exports financed by capital exports) has been argued by Arthur Lewis.[25] It is also significant that the period of the inter-War years, when capital exports dried up owing to uncertainties of exchange rate movements (or, some might say,[26] the 'closing of the frontier', since much of the capital exports were to the temperate regions of white settlement), also saw the greatest depression in the history of capitalism: the over-production crisis, it can be argued, which had been suppressed through capital exports till then suddenly burst forth.

Not only are all these historically plausible arguments, but they have actually been made by a host of Marxist or progressive economists and economic historians. They deserve serious attention from any student of capitalism. But the important point is this: neither under-consumption, nor under-investment constitutes a part of Lenin's argument. John Strachey however interpreted Lenin as providing an under-consumptionist argument. Having done so, he then proceeded to critique Lenin's theory

[23] R. Prebisch, *The Economic Development of Latin America and its Principal Problems*, UNECLA, 1950; W.A. Lewis, *Growth and Fluctuations 1870–1913*, London, 1978.

[24] E.J. Hobsbawm, *Industry and Empire*, Harmondsworth: Penguin, 1969.

[25] W.A. Lewis, *Economic Survey 1919–1939*, London, 1949.

[26] This group would include J.M. Keynes, *Economic Consequences of the Peace*, London, 1919.

on the grounds that Keynesian demand management policies had made it unnecessary to resort to capital exports for warding off any tendency towards over-production.

This however is not Lenin's theory (though it figures prominently in Hobson). There may be a tendency towards generalized over-production under monopoly capitalism, either from under-consumption in any of the ways suggested above (as a host of Marxist writers from Kalecki to Baran and Sweezy were to argue later) or from under-investment (in the manner outlined above). But Lenin's theory does not invoke any such tendency *because it is not a functional theory of imperialism at all.* Let us therefore look briefly at his argument.

The competition between capitals, which is the hallmark of capitalism, takes the form of rivalries between large monopoly combines, aided by their respective nation-states, in the era of monopoly capitalism. As a part of this rivalry each monopoly combine tries to acquire for itself as much of 'economic territory' as possible, as sources of raw material, as markets, as destinations of capital exports, and quite often for no reason other than to prevent its falling into the hands of its rivals. Imperialism, in other words, is not some specially designed policy to serve a functional necessity. It is endemic to monopoly capitalism. It is not a thing apart but simply the way monopoly capitalism behaves, which is why distinguishing it from monopoly capitalism is misleading.

Once this is recognized, a number of criticisms of Lenin's theory appear altogether misdirected. The first of these is the criticism advanced by Strachey that was mentioned earlier, namely that Keynesian demand management policies which came into vogue in the post-War period made Lenin's theory of imperialism obsolete. This criticism, which presumes that Lenin's theory was based on under-consumptionism, lacks validity. It does not address at all the basic proposition of Lenin on monopoly capitalism.

A second, related, criticism which shares the same presumption as the first, proceeds as follows: capital exports can provide additional demand for the imperialist economies as a whole only if they are made to 'outside' economies, i.e., to the colonies, the dependencies and the backward economies. In other words, if imperialism were a means of warding off generalized over-production in the advanced capitalist economies, then it must entail capital exports from the advanced to the backward economies. As a matter of fact, however, the bulk of the capital exports historically have been among the advanced countries themselves, which constitutes a refutation of Lenin's theory. The refutation becomes even stronger when we take the net flows: these net flows to the backward economies were in fact negative since the capital exports to them were in general less than the surplus drained out of them during the period that Lenin was writing about. This criticism too, however, is invalid, since Lenin was not seeing imperialism as a functional necessity to ward off generalized over-production.[27]

This last argument is often expressed in a slightly different way. If capital exports were undertaken from the advanced countries to ward off over-production, then they would have to be made to the backward economies; this would lead to a diffusion of industrial capitalism where the difference between the developed and the underdeveloped economies would disappear. Since this distinction has not disappeared, Lenin's theory which (allegedly) predicted such capital exports is wrong. This criticism is obviously invalid. Seeing Lenin as a crude 'diffusionist' is simply an extension of seeing him as an under-consumptionist.

A third criticism springs from the same misunderstanding. This states that Lenin kept giving figures about the stock of capital exported while what was needed for the substantiation of his theory was the flow of capital exports in each period. He therefore confused stocks with flows, and misread into the stock figures, claims that should have been substantiated from the flow figures. Once again this criticism assumes that Lenin's theory believed imperialism to be a way of preventing over-production through capital exports. In fact Lenin's perception of imperialism was altogether different. And while he drew pointed attention to capital exports as characterizing imperialism, he saw neither imperialism nor even capital exports in functional terms at all.

Finally, even Karl Kautsky's criticism of a theoretical trend (of which Lenin was a later example) on the definition of imperialism springs from the same error of interpretation. Kautsky's argument was that if imperialism is defined as present-day capitalism, if it is seen merely as

---

[27] In addition, as mentioned above, much of the capital exports occurred anyway to the so-called 'frontiers', i.e. to the temperate regions of white settlement, which, only through this process, get 'internalized' by the capitalist world.

being constituted by 'all the phenomena of present-day capitalism', then the question of whether it is necessary for capitalism becomes reduced to the 'flattest tautology', because then 'imperialism is naturally a vital necessity for capitalism'. Kautsky's insistence that the necessity of imperialism for capitalism be separately established is tantamount to an insistence on a functional theory of imperialism. There is no reason however why imperialism should be seen in purely functional terms. On the contrary, as Lenin was to point out, underlying this insistence is a view of imperialism as a 'preferred policy', i.e., a belief that alternative policies are possible *on the same economic basis of trusts and cartels.*

V

There can be scarcely any doubt that Lenin's prognostications in *Imperialism* were resoundingly vindicated during the period 1914–45. The real question however is: what is the relationship between the Leninist perception and the post-Second World War developments when capitalism is supposed to have 'changed'?

Capitalism emerged from the Second World War badly bruised. The balance of class forces in the advanced capitalist countries had shifted quite significantly in favour of the working class, which had made immense sacrifices during the War. And the tide of the national liberation struggle in the colonies had swollen to a torrent. Capitalism pursued in this situation a two-pronged strategy for its immediate survival: isolation and repression of the revolutionary forces, notably the Communists, on the one hand; and concessions to and compromises with the demands of the domestic working class and the colonial movements. The Cold War, the rise of McCarthyism, the suppression of the revolutionary struggles in Greece and Malaya, the attempted suppression of the struggles in Vietnam and Korea (and through the latter the attempt to hit back at China where the imperialist-supported Kuomintang had proved unequal to the task of defeating the Communists), the removal from the post-War coalition governments of the French and the Italian Communists who had acquired immense popularity because of their role in the Resistance, and the string of military bases set up all over the world by the US, were all examples of the first track of this two-pronged strategy. There can be little doubt that an important element underlying the successes that imperialism had on this front was the fact that the United States had emerged relatively unscathed from the War while the Soviet Union had borne the brunt of the War and had been its worst sufferer.

It is the second track of this strategy however that concerns us here. That involved decolonization by handing power wherever possible to the emerging Third World bourgeoisie; the introduction of Keynesian demand management policies to achieve near-full employment at home; and the provision of a host of welfare measures (though much of it was paid for by the working class itself).[28] These concessions together created a conjuncture that proved highly favourable to growth, and the capitalist world experienced the most impressive boom in its history during the decades of the fifties and the sixties.

Three elements went into this boom: first, the high levels of demand sustained through Keynesian demand management, and in particular the large US budget deficits, incurred *inter alia* for financing the massive military expenditure bill, ensured that investment, and with it the growth rate, was kept up. Secondly, the stock of innovations not introduced during the inter-War period marked by Depression, was available for introduction now, together with a host of new innovations that resulted in part from the War-time technological advances.[29] And these kept up the rate of productivity growth, owing to which the workers could obtain significant wage increases in the prevailing conditions of high employment. Thirdly, in their bid to step up the pace of industrialization through the imports of capital goods, the newly-independent Third World countries vied with one another for pushing out primary commodity exports, so that notwithstanding decolonization the terms of trade for primary commodities deteriorated *vis-à-vis* manufacturing. This contributed to keeping inflation rates low in the metropolis and hence prolonging the boom.[30]

In the course of the boom the working class in the metropolis therefore made significant gains in terms of its living standards. The Third World as a whole also grew much faster than ever in its history. Within the

---

[28] On this last point see my essay, 'On the Economic Crisis of World Capitalism' in *Lenin and Imperialism*.

[29] This point has been made by Lewis, *Growth and Fluctuations 1870–1913*.

[30] For a detailed discussion of this last argument as well as for data and explanations of terms of trade movements, see my book *Accumulation and Stability Under Capitalism*, Oxford: Clarendon Press, 1997.

Third World, moreover, some countries which for geo-political reasons (as 'frontline states' in the fight against Communism) were accorded generous market access by the metropolitan countries, grew particularly rapidly. Both these phenomena created the impression that capitalism had 'changed'. Henceforth, it was argued, we would have the reign of 'welfare capitalism' in the metropolis within which the working class would continue to prosper. As regards the Third World, being 'linked' to the metropolitan countries, such as East and South-East Asian countries were linked, no longer appeared to constitute a barrier to economic advance (contrary to the formulation of the Sixth Congress of the Comintern, which was widely believed by even non-Marxist Third World nationalists).

In retrospect however, the entire period of the post-War boom, 'welfarism', and successful diffusion of industrial capitalism to the Third World, which appeared to negate Marxist prognostications, seems like an exception, a discontinuity, a displacement of the system brought about by the exigencies of the post-War situation rather than the 'normal' functioning of the system. Indeed the very tendencies of capitalism highlighted by Lenin, notably centralization of capital, operating through the boom years, have brought about not only the end of this phase of capitalism but even a rolling back of the achievements of the metropolitan working class and the Third World peoples. Capitalism since the seventies has acquired an altogether different, though more familiar look (in terms of its predatoriness, its inhumaneness, and its attempt to dominate). This of course does not mean that we have a return to the conjuncture that prevailed in the pre-War period and that was captured so aptly and superbly by the Leninist vision. It means the unfolding of a new conjuncture, some words on which may be in order.

VI

Centralization of capital today has proceeded much beyond what Lenin had written about. What is more, it has not proceeded within the parameters of the world described by Lenin but by transcending those parameters. It is not the case that German capital *qua* German capital has got more centralized, or British capital *qua* British capital has got more centralized, and that each has remained locked in rivalry with the other in the manner described by Lenin. Rather, the centralization of capital within each has been accompanied and overlaid by a process of 'globalization' of capital (in a specific sense that I shall describe shortly) that has transcended these rivalries themselves. Centralization has not meant mere quantitative changes in a world frozen in the same mould as in Lenin's time. It has meant a qualitative transformation in the world itself.

Of course globalization of capital *per se* is not a new phenomenon; it cannot be. There was globalization of capital in Lenin's time as well, since imperialism necessarily entails such globalization. Contemporary globalization however has certain specific characteristics which emerge with sharper relief when we compare it to what was happening at the turn of the century. In the heyday of capital exports prior to the First World War, Britain, the leading capital exporter of that time, ran a current account surplus of between 5 and 10 per cent of her GNP for over four decades, averaging 8 per cent over the two decades prior to the War. By contrast the largest capital exporter of modern times, Japan, has run current account surpluses averaging only 2.8 per cent of her GDP during the decade 1984–93.[31] What this shows is *not* that capital flows today are relatively less important than earlier, but that such flows are largely detached from the current account of the balance of payments, i.e., they pertain largely to the capital account of the balance of payments. Now, direct foreign investment, or other long-term capital flows generally give rise to concomitant commodity movements as well, which are reflected in the current account of the balance of payments. On the other hand, short-term financial flows, which represent pure shifting of funds from one form of asset holding to another, do not generate concomitant commodity movements (except when they precipitate a crisis). The fact that contemporary capital flows are associated with relatively small current account surpluses by the leading capital exporters therefore is indicative of the fact that much of this capital movement represents short-run speculative capital flows. Direct confirmation of this is provided by the fact that only about 2 per cent of cross-border capital flows is on account of trade related transactions. In short, 'globalization' today is not accompanied by any significant relative increase in long-term capital flows; it represents predominantly a globalization of

---

[31] These figures are taken from Jayati Ghosh and Abhijit Sen, 'Capital Flows and Macro-Economies: A Historical View' in *Economics as Ideology and Experience: Essays in Honour of Ashok Mitra*, edited by Deepak Nayyar, London: Frank Cass, 1998.

finance in the form of 'hot money' flows. It is not the mobility of capital-in-production that has increased in relative terms, but the mobility of capital-as-finance. When we talk of finance capital today we refer to an entity that is quite different from the finance capital of Lenin's days.

At least three differences need to be noted. First, Lenin had talked about nation-based, and hence nation-state aided, finance capital; what we have today is finance which, though drawn from particular nations, is neither amenable to the control or discipline of any nation-state, nor engaged in promoting any definable 'national interest'. Secondly, and correspondingly, we do not have the coalescence of industry and finance (both based in a particular nation and aided by the particular nation-state) that Bukharin had talked about and Lenin had endorsed. Instead what we have is finance pursuing its objectives, which predominantly amount to making speculative gains through 'hot money' flows. Thirdly, this finance operates not in the context of intense inter-imperialist rivalries, but rather in the context of very noticeable unity among the leading capitalist powers. This is not to say that rivalries among them do not exist; of course they do and could even flare up some day, even to the point of resembling what Lenin had written about. But, as of now, and especially *vis-à-vis* the Third World countries, they display a remarkable degree of unity.

These differences from Lenin's picture of finance capital are not matters for mere cataloguing. They are themselves interrelated; and they conjure up an altogether different totality. For example, globalized capital as a block cannot be too closely tethered to industry based in a particular imperialist country: the very fact of it being globalized implies that it has to spill out of the narrow confines of industry and pursue a whole lot of activities in search of quick gains, which make it predominantly speculative in character. Likewise its very global character is an important factor that keeps inter-imperialist rivalries in check. Any fragmentation of the world into separate 'spheres of influence', which would happen under intensified inter-imperialist rivalry, would put barriers in the way of global movements of finance. The traits we have underscored, in other words, fit into one another, and they define an altogether new entity.

At the same time, it must not be forgotten that this globalization of finance is based on and itself represents an enormous unprecedented centralization, a carrying forward of precisely the process that Lenin had emphasised. In fact, today not only do we have centralization of finance capital in the usual sense of financial institutions controlling and deploying enormous amounts of funds, but also in the additional sense of their being able to stimulate 'herd behaviour' among others in response to their own actions, so that they also influence the decisions of finance that is not under their direct control. The entire globe is the theatre of operation of this gigantic block (in the sense of being inclined to move synchronously) of finance, which though drawn from specific countries is no longer in any narrow sense 'tied' to the 'national interest'. In the sphere of finance we thus have globalization accompanying centralization, which has reached such a level that a single credit-rating agency, or a single George Soros, can wreck an economy within hours by causing capital flight out of it.

Emphasizing this aspect of globalization of finance should not give the impression that the centralization of capital in the sphere of production, in the form of multinational corporations and their global activities is of secondary importance. But much is written about the MNCs which have also been with us for a long time now. Globalization of finance, by contrast, is a relatively more recent phenomenon of great consequence, and hence deserves special attention.

The consequences of the process of centralization-cum-globaliz-ation of finance capital are quite far-reaching. First, it is one contributory factor to the prolonged slowdown in the advanced capitalist world and the high unemployment rates that prevail (on which cyclical crises are additionally superimposed). No doubt the impact of this slowdown has been uneven across the advanced capitalist countries, with Britain and the United States doing rather better than the rest (on which more later). No doubt there are other important contributory factors to the slowdown, but the role of this particular factor cannot be underestimated.

It restricts the scope for demand management by the nation-state, undermining Keynesianism directly. Financial interests within any country, as Keynes and Kalecki had argued, tend to be hostile to demand manage-ment: when finance is *international* this hostility acquires a spontaneous effectiveness. Any effort by the state to expand economic activity makes speculators apprehensive about inflation, exchange rate depreciation, and, more generally, of political radicalism, and finance flows out of the country. This precipitates actual depreciation and inflation, forcing the state to curtail activity to some level that speculators feel comfortable with. Putting it differently, state intervention presupposes a 'control area' of the state over which its writ can run; 'globalization' of finance tends to undermine this 'control area'.

The fact that a host of left-wing governments in the advanced capitalist countries, elected on the promise that they would increase employment, have signally failed to do so, underscores this objective constraint on state intervention. This constraint also explains the decline of all ideologies of social change, from social democracy to Keynesianism to Third World nationalism: since all of them see the nation-state as the agency of intervention, whereas the 'globalization' of finance, by restricting the state's capacity to intervene, has undermined their coherence. Indeed, the decline of the Soviet Union too is not unrelated to this phenomenon of 'globalization' of finance, since even the Soviet system had towards the end lost its immunity to capital flights.

The levels of activity and employment in the advanced capitalist world as a whole would not be so low, even without state intervention in demand management in individual countries, if the US state could boost aggregate demand for all of them. One would normally expect that the dollar being the strongest currency, even without the *imprimatur* of the Bretton Woods system, the US would play this 'leadership' role for the capitalist world as a whole by enlarging its fiscal and current account deficits. Paradoxically the US too is not free of the need to appease international finance capital. It has curtailed its fiscal deficit, and to a lesser extent its current account deficit in real terms. As a consequence finance has flowed into the US and Britain (the Anglo-Saxon world in any case is the traditional home of finance) causing some expansion in these economies through finance-related activities. The rest of the capitalist world has been doomed to stagnation. This may well react back at some later stage on the US and Britain, converting the current protracted but partial stagnation of the capitalist world into a generalized one.

Secondly, this new context has resulted in the unleashing of a major imperialist offensive against the Third World, in the form of the imposition of 'liberalization'. The prising open of Third World markets for goods and services helps in overcoming metropolitan stagnation. While doing so, moreover, it is particularly advantageous for two reasons: first, it keeps at bay state intervention in demand management, and with it any 'threat' of political radicalism; second, by de-industrializing the Third World and generally forcing it into greater reliance on primary production, it keeps inflationary pressures in the metropolis in check.

Of even greater importance however is the prising open of the Third World to the unrestricted movements of international finance capital. This not only expands the area over which speculative gains can be made, but also brings a wealth of mineral resources and major industrial enterprises, especially public sector enterprises which are forced to be privatized 'for a song', under the potential control of finance capital. 'Liberalization' in short is a mechanism for the further centralization of capital on a world scale: metropolitan capital-in-production ousts Third World producers, while metropolitan capital-as-finance (which is the dominant component of 'globalized' finance) gets control over Third World resources and enterprises built up earlier at public cost, at throwaway prices.

The emergence of international finance capital therefore is associated with a new epoch which differs in very significant ways both from the epoch that Lenin had written about, and from the immediate post-War period of capitalist boom and welfarism. While the first difference would be appreciated by many, this second difference is less appreciated up to now.

VII

The fact that globalization of finance capital has brought about a degree of unity among the imperialist countries, at least in their dealings with the Third World, may create the impression that the world has moved to the Kautskyan vision of 'ultra-imperialism' rather than remaining submerged in 'inter-imperialist rivalries' as Lenin had prognosticated, that real developments have vindicated Kautsky rather than Lenin. To believe this, however, would constitute a serious misreading not only of the basic difference between Lenin and Kautsky but also of contemporary reality.

After a period of unquestioned US hegemony (or what some have called 'super-imperialism'), characterized *inter alia* by the Bretton Woods arrangement which proclaimed the dollar to be 'as good as gold', it appeared in the seventies as if there would be a revival of inter-imperialist rivalry. There is no doubt however that imperialist countries managed to keep this rivalry within check, which is why they could impose the 'liberalization' package upon the Third World through the three institutions they dominate: the IMF, the World Bank, and the WTO. There is also no doubt, as suggested earlier, that this unity subsists upon the fact of globalization of capital in a new incarnation which might approximate the Kautskyan notion of 'internationally-united finance capital'. Capital needs the backing of the state, and if capital is mobile all over the world then it needs the backing of some state whose jurisdiction runs all over the world. In the absence of a world-state, the only agency that can provide this backing, especially if capital itself happens to be a composite block drawn from different nations, is the imperialist states acting unitedly (under a clear leadership which of course can come only from the US). But this very fact, which appears to vindicate Kautsky, paradoxically reveals the weakness of his position.[32]

The difference between Kautsky and Lenin was not a scholastic one relating to whether the finance capitals of the different imperialist countries would remain united or divided. The difference related to the question of war and peace. Lenin was categorical that

> the real social significance of Kautsky's 'theory' is this: it is a most reactionary method of consoling the masses with hopes of permanent peace being possible under capitalism, by distracting their attention from the sharp antagonisms and acute problems of the present times, and directing it towards illusory prospects of an imaginary 'ultra-imperialism' of the future.[33]

The fact that the question of war and peace was at the centre of the difference between Lenin and Kautsky, and that this in turn was intimately linked to the question of revolution is made clear by Lenin in the following remark:

> Historically and economically speaking, they [i.e. the 'Centrists'] are not a *separate* stratum but represent only a *transition* from a past phase of the working class movement – the phase between 1871 and 1914, which gave much that is valuable to the proletariat, particularly in the indispensable art of slow, sustained and

---

[32] The argument which follows has gained greatly from Amiya Kumar Bagchi's 'Towards a Correct Reading of Lenin's Theory of Imperialism' in *Lenin and Imperialism*.

[33] *Selected Works*, volume 1, p. 723.

systematic organizational work on a large and very large scale – to a new *phase* that became *objectively* essential with the outbreak of the first imperialist war, which inaugurated *the era of social revolution.*[34]

It is the War, an inevitable outcome of imperialism, which inaugurates the era of social revolution. Kautsky's 'ultra-imperialist fable' is 'reactionary' because it seeks to hide this fact that we are in an era of social revolution by denying the inevitability of war in the epoch of imperialism. This is the thrust of Lenin's criticism.

'Ultra-imperialism' thus was repugnant to Lenin because it conjured up a vision of global peace under capitalism (and *ipso facto* denied the fact that social revolution had come on the agenda). And it is this vision that he attacked. The line of his attack was as follows: uneven development under capitalism necessarily implies that any agreement among the imperialist powers for the joint exploitation of the world, which is based on their prevailing relative strengths, gets undermined over time; a redrawing of the agreement is achieved through the use of force. Conflicts and struggles among the imperialist powers, even if interrupted by periods of truce, are a perennial feature. Peaceful periods are mere interludes of temporary truce; permanent peace under capitalism is impossible.

The current unity among the imperialist powers too may prove to be only transient. What is more, *even if this unity lasts,* i.e., even if inter-imperialist conflicts remain muted, this still does not mean that wars would have been avoided, since other kinds of wars would break out to disrupt the 'joint exploitation of the world by internationally-united finance capital'. One obvious example would be wars between united imperialism and countries unwilling to toe its line. In fact Lenin himself in his writings after *Imperialism* cited wars of several different kinds, in addition to inter-imperialist conflicts, as being a necessary occurrence in the era of imperialism. In our own time, during the current decade alone, notwithstanding imperialist unity, in spite of the collapse of the Soviet Union, and notwithstanding the fact that struggles within the Third World against the new phase of imperialism are still at a nascent stage, there have nonetheless

---

[34] *Collected Works,* volume 24, pp. 76–77. Italics in the original.

been two wars, unleashed by imperialism against Iraq and Yugoslavia, which only underscore this point.

The current process of 'globalization' of capital has disastrous consequences for the Third World; and such consequences would necessarily beget conflicts and wars. At least five consequences are relevant here. First, it entails a drastic squeeze on the living standards of the workers and peasants in the Third World. Trade liberalization has the effect of de-industrializing these economies and pushing them into export agriculture which is both detrimental to their food security and exposes the peasants to the vicissitudes of sharp price fluctuations on the world market. Getting caught in the vortex of international finance has the effect of trapping them into being perennially concerned about retaining the 'confidence' of international speculators; for this they keep interest rates high, government expenditure restricted, subsidies lowered, the economy deflated and workers' rights curtailed. The net effect of all this is stagnation, higher unemployment, and a regressive shift in income distribution, which together accentuate poverty.

Secondly, it abrogates the economic and political sovereignty of these countries. The unhindered operation within these countries of international capital that is dominated by and mediated through the metropolis, requires such an abrogation, since protection for such capital has to be arranged by metropolitan states, and agencies like the IMF controlled by them, by subverting the autonomy of the Third World states. But holding these countries under the thraldom of IMF conditionalities, which is the obvious mechanism for subverting autonomy, is usually supplemented by other mechanisms. As a part of the measures to retain 'investors' confidence', key positions in government have often got to be handed over to pro-imperialist politicians and bureaucrats. Personnel from the Fund and the Bank are deployed in the economic ministries which in turn are given greater autonomy on the plea of preventing them from being hamstrung by the caprices of the 'politicians'. (Autonomy of the central bank of course is insisted upon as a part of financial liberalization itself). All these measures ensure that economic decision-making cannot be undertaken in an autonomous fashion by the domestic state.

Thirdly, associated with the effort to retain 'investors' confidence' is a progressive transfer of natural resources and assets, especially of the public sector, to foreign hands at throwaway prices, a process of what one may call 'denationalization'. 'Privatization' in any case is imposed on these economies as a part of IMF conditionalities, and the beneficiaries of it are, eventually if not immediately, the MNCs. In addition, whenever the caprices of international speculators threaten a capital flight, the government in desperation resorts to denationalization of valuable assets, as a means of checking it.

Fourthly, since the abrogation of sovereignty, the squeeze on the working people, the transfer of precious domestic assets 'for a song' to foreign hands, cannot be effected without reducing the political power of the people, there is necessarily an attenuation of democracy. There are several mechanisms for this, including some that have been mentioned above. But a very powerful mechanism consists in the following: different bourgeois and petty bourgeois political parties, afraid of triggering off capital flight, swear allegiance to the same set of policies of 'liberalization', so that the people are denied any effective political choice. In short, satisfying the caprices of international speculators on the one hand and respecting the will of the people on the other, are mutually incompatible; once the economy, and by implication the polity, gets oriented towards satisfying the former, it has perforce to find ways of circumventing the latter.

Finally, these countries become inevitably enmeshed in ethnic conflicts, secessionist movements, communal conflagrations, and fundamentalist threats once they 'liberalize' their economies and get caught in the vortex of international financial flows. Deflation and unemployment are conducive to the growth of exclusivist and chauvinist movements of various kinds, as the break up of Yugoslavia has clearly demonstrated. Such internecine struggles not only engulf Third World societies once they have adopted the imperialist-dictated policies, but are particularly useful from the point of view of imperialism: they act as a barrier to the emergence of revolutionary challenges to imperialism by dividing the people; they permit an effective whittling down of democracy; and they permit imperialism to intervene whenever it likes in the name of 'preventing human rights abuses' (NATO of course has now openly declared that it can intervene if 'economic reforms' are threatened, but championing 'human rights' is more easily saleable).

VIII

The net result of all these accentuated contradictions is that conflicts and wars of diverse kinds continue even in this phase of greater imperialist unity. These in turn produce from time to time conjunctures that are favourable for the advance of the anti-imperialist struggles in particular countries.[35] Preserving the gains that are made during such advances in particular countries, linking these advances across countries, building bridges between these struggles and the struggles of the working class in the metropolis where unemployment, stagnation and welfare cuts have become endemic, require a new theoretical advance which alone can provide the basis for the correct formulation of strategy and tactics. In short, there is need today to fill a theoretical void by reconstructing Marxism, much as Lenin's *Imperialism* had done in its time. For doing so, however, Lenin's *Imperialism* itself must first be thoroughly studied and understood. The purpose of bringing out the text which follows is precisely to aid this study and understanding.

[35] Such advance of course would require the formulation of appropriate transitional programmes for the Third World societies by the revolutionary forces opposed to imperialism. A discussion of the contents of such programmes is outside the scope of the present Introduction. A brief outline of the *economic* component of such a programme is given in Prabhat Patnaik and C.P. Chandrashekhar, 'India: *Dirigisme*, Structural Adjustment and the Radical Alternative', in *Globalization and Progressive Economic Policy*, edited by Dean Baker et al., Cambridge: CUP, 1998.

PREFACE

The pamphlet here presented to the reader was written in the spring of 1916, in Zurich. In the conditions in which I was obliged to work there I naturally suffered somewhat from a shortage of French and English literature and from a serious dearth of Russian literature. However, I made use of the principal English work on imperialism, the book by J.A. Hobson, with all the care that, in my opinion that work deserves.

This pamphlet was written with an eye to the tsarist censorship. Hence, I was not only forced to confine myself strictly to an exclusively theoretical, specifically economic analysis of facts, but to formulate the few necessary observations on politics with extreme caution, by hints, in an allegorical language – in that accursed Aesopian language – to which tsarism compelled all revolutionaries to have recourse whenever they took up the pen to write a 'legal' work.

It is painful, in these days of liberty, to re-read the passages of the pamphlet which have been distorted, cramped, compressed in an iron vice on account of the censor. That the period of imperialism is the eve of the socialist revolution; that social-chauvinism (socialism in words, chauvinism in deeds) is the utter betrayal of socialism, complete desertion to the side of the bourgeoisie; that this split in the working-class movement is bound up with the objective conditions of imperialism, etc. – on these matters I had to speak in a 'slavish' tongue, and I must refer the reader who is interested in the subject to the articles I wrote abroad in 1914–17, a new edition of which is soon to appear. Special attention should be drawn to a passage on pages 119–20.[1] In order to show the reader, in a guise acceptable to the censors, how shamelessly untruthful the capitalists and the social-chauvinists who have deserted to their side (and whom Kautsky opposes so inconsistently) are on the question of annexations; in order to show how shamelessly they *screen* the annexations of *their* capitalists, I was forced to quote as an example – Japan! The careful reader will easily substitute Russia for Japan, and Finland, Poland, Courland, the Ukraine, Khiva, Bokhara, Estonia or other regions peopled by non-Great Russians, for Korea.

I trust that this pamphlet will help the reader to understand the fundamental economic question, that of the economic essence of imperialism, for unless this is studied, it will be impossible to understand and appraise modern war and modern politics.

Petrograd. April 26, 1917   AUTHOR

---

[1] See p. 145 of the present volume.

PREFACE TO THE FRENCH AND GERMAN EDITIONS

I

As was indicated in the preface to the Russian edition, this pamphlet was written in 1916, with an eye to the tsarist censorship. I am unable to revise the whole text at the present time, nor, perhaps, would this be advisable, since the main purpose of the book was, and remains, to present, on the basis of the summarized returns of irrefutable bourgeois statistics, and the admissions of bourgeois scholars of all countries, *a composite picture* of the world capitalist system in its international relationships at the beginning of the twentieth century – on the eve of the first world imperialist war.

    To a certain extent it will even be useful for many Communists in advanced capitalist countries to convince themselves by the example of this pamphlet, *legal from the standpoint of the tsarist censor*, of the possibility, and necessity, of making use of even the slight remnants of legality which still remain at the disposal of the Communists, say, in contemporary America or France, after the recent almost wholesale arrests of Communists, in order to explain the utter falsity of social-pacifist views and hopes for 'world democracy'. The most essential of what should be added to this censored pamphlet I shall try to present in this preface.

II

It is proved in the pamphlet that the war of 1914–18 was imperialist (that is, an annexationist, predatory, war of plunder) on the part of both sides; it was a war for the division of the world, for the partition and repartition of colonies and spheres of influence of finance capital, etc.

Proof of what was the true social, or rather, the true class character of the war is naturally to be found, not in the diplomatic history of the war, but in an analysis of the *objective* position of the ruling *classes* in *all* the belligerent countries. In order to depict this objective position one must not take examples or isolated data (in view of the extreme complexity of the phenomena of social life it is always possible to select any number of examples or separate data to prove any proposition), but *all* the data on the *basis* of economic life in *all* the belligerent countries and the *whole* world.

It is precisely irrefutable summarized data of this kind that I quoted in describing the *partition of the world* in 1876 and 1914 (in Chapter VI) and the division of the world's *railways* in 1890 and 1913 (in Chapter VII). Railways are a summation of the basic capitalist industries, coal, iron and steel; a summation and the most striking index of the development of world trade and bourgeois-democratic civilization. How the railways are linked up with large-scale industry, with monopolies, syndicates, cartels, trusts, banks and the financial oligarchy is shown in the preceding chapters of the book. The uneven distribution of the railways, their uneven development – sums up, as it were, modern monopolist capitalism on a world-wide scale. And this summary proves that imperialist wars are absolutely inevitable under *such* an economic system, *as long as* private property in the means of production exists.

The building of railways seems to be a simple, natural, democratic, cultural and civilizing enterprise; that is what it is in the opinion of the bourgeois professors who are paid to depict capitalist slavery in bright colours, and in the opinion of petty-bourgeois philistines. But as a matter of fact the capitalist threads, which in thousands of different intercrossings bind these enterprises with private property in the means of production in general, have converted this railway construction into an instrument for oppressing *a thousand million* people (in the colonies and semi-colonies), that is, more than half the population of the globe that inhabits the dependent countries, as well as the wage-slaves of capital in the 'civilized' countries.

Private property based on the labour of the small proprietor, free competition, democracy, all the catchwords with which the capitalists and their press deceive the workers and the peasants – are things of the distant past. Capitalism has grown into a world system of colonial oppression and of the financial strangulation of the overwhelming majority of the population of the world by a handful of 'advanced' countries. And this 'booty' is shared between two or three powerful world plunderers armed to the teeth (America, Great Britain, Japan), who are drawing the whole world into *their* war over the division of *their* booty.

III

The Treaty of Brest-Litovsk dictated by monarchist Germany, and the subsequent much more brutal and despicable Treaty of Versailles dictated by the 'democratic' republics of America and France and also by 'free' Britain, have rendered a most useful service to humanity by exposing both imperialism's hired coolies of the pen and petty-bourgeois reactionaries who, although they call themselves pacifists and socialists, sang praises to 'Wilsonism', and insisted that peace and reforms were possible under imperialism.

The tens of millions of dead and maimed left by the war – a war to decide whether the British or German group of financial plunderers is to receive the most booty – and those two 'peace treaties', are with unprecedented rapidity opening the eyes of the millions and tens of millions of people who are downtrodden, oppressed, deceived and duped by the bourgeoisie. Thus, out of the universal ruin caused by the war a worldwide revolutionary crisis is arising which, however prolonged and arduous its stages may be, cannot end otherwise than in a proletarian revolution and in its victory.

The Basle Manifesto of the Second International, which in 1912 gave an appraisal of the very war that broke out in 1914 and not of war in general (there are different kinds of wars, including revolutionary wars) – this Manifesto is now a monument exposing to the full the shameful bankruptcy and treachery of the heroes of the Second International.

That is why I reproduce this Manifesto as a supplement to the present edition, and again and again I urge the reader to note that the heroes of the Second International are as assiduously avoiding the passages of this Manifesto which speak precisely, clearly and definitely of the connection between that impending war and the proletarian revolution, as a thief avoids the scene of his crime.

IV

Special attention has been devoted in this pamphlet to a criticism of Kautskyism, the international ideological trend represented in all countries of the world by the 'most prominent theoreticians', the leaders of the Second International (Otto Bauer and Co. in Austria, Ramsay MacDonald and others in Britain, Albert Thomas in France, etc., etc.) and a multitude of socialists, reformists, pacifists, bourgeois democrats and parsons.

This ideological trend is, on the one hand, a product of the disintegration and decay of the Second International, and, on the hand, the inevitable fruit of the ideology of the petty bourgeoisie, whose entire way of life holds them captive to bourgeois and democratic prejudices.

The views held by Kautsky and his like are a complete renunciation of those same revolutionary principles of Marxism that writer has championed for decades, especially, by the way, in his struggle against socialist opportunism (of Bernstein, Millerand, Hyndman, Gompers, etc.). It is not a mere accident, therefore, that Kautsky's followers all over the world have now united in practical politics with the extreme opportunists (through the Second, or Yellow International) and with the bourgeois governments (through bourgeois coalition governments in which socialists take part).

The growing world proletarian revolutionary movement in general, and the communist movement in particular, cannot dispense with an analysis and exposure of the theoretical errors of Kautskyism. The more so since pacifism and 'democracy' in general, which lay no claim to Marxism whatever, but which, like Kautsky and Co., are obscuring the profundity of the contradictions of imperialism and the inevitable revolutionary crisis to which it gives rise, are still very widespread all over the world. To combat these tendencies is the bounden duty of the party of the proletariat, which must win away from the bourgeoisie the small proprietors who are duped by them, and the millions of working people who enjoy more or less petty-bourgeois conditions of life.

V

A few words must be said about Chapter VIII, 'Parasitism and Decay of Capitalism'. As already pointed out in the text, Hilferding, ex-'Marxist', and now a comrade-in-arms of Kautsky and one of the chief exponents of bourgeois, reformist policy in the Independent Social-Democratic Party of Germany, has taken a step backward on this question compared with the *frankly* pacifist and reformist Englishman, Hobson. The international split of the entire working-class movement is now quite evident (the Second and the Third Internationals). The fact that armed struggle and civil war is now raging between the two trends is also evident – the support given to Kolchak and Denikin in Russia by the Mensheviks and Socialist-Revolutionaries against the Bolsheviks; the fight the Scheidemanns and Noskes have conducted in conjunction with the bourgeoisie against the Spartacists in Germany; the same thing in Finland, Poland, Hungary, etc. What is the economic basis of this world-historical phenomenon?

It is precisely the parasitism and decay of capitalism, characteristic of its highest historical stage of development, i.e., imperialism. As this pamphlet shows, capitalism has now singled out a *handful* (less than one-tenth of the inhabitants of the globe; less than one-fifth at a most 'generous' and liberal calculation) of exceptionally rich and powerful states which plunder the whole world simply by 'clipping coupons'. Capital exports yield an income of eight to ten thousand million francs per annum, at pre-war prices and according to pre-war bourgeois statistics. Now, of course, they yield much more.

Obviously, out of such enormous *superprofits* (since they are obtained over and above the profits which capitalists squeeze out of the workers of their 'own' country) it is *possible to bribe* the labour leaders and the upper stratum of the labour aristocracy. And that is just what the capitalists of the 'advanced' countries are doing: they are bribing them in a thousand different ways, direct and indirect, overt and covert.

This stratum of workers-turned-bourgeois, or the labour aristocracy, who are quite philistine in their mode of life, in the size of their earnings and in their entire outlook, is the principal prop of the Second International, and in our days, the principal *social* (not military) *prop of the bourgeoisie*. For they are the real *agents of the bourgeoisie in the working-class* movement, the labour lieutenants of the capitalist class, real vehicles of reformism and chauvinism. In the civil war between the proletariat and the bourgeoisie they inevitably, and in no small numbers, take the side of the bourgeoisie, the 'Versaillais' against the 'Communards'.

Unless the economic roots of this phenomenon are understood and its political and social significance is appreciated, not a step can be taken toward the solution of the practical problems of the communist movement and of the impending social revolution.

Imperialism is the eve of the social revolution of the proletariat. This has been confirmed since 1917 on a world-wide scale.

July 6, 1920   N. LENIN

During the last
fifteen to twenty years, especially since the Spanish–American War (1898) and the Anglo–Boer War (1899–1902), the economic and also the political literature of the two hemispheres has more and more often adopted the term 'imperialism' in order to describe the present era. In 1902, a book by the English economist J.A. Hobson, *Imperialism*, was published in London and New York. This author, whose point of view is that of bourgeois social-reformism and pacifism which, in essence, is identical with the present point of view of the ex-Marxist, Karl Kautsky, gives a very good and comprehensive description of the principal specific economic and political features of imperialism. In 1910, there appeared in Vienna the work of the Austrian Marxist, Rudolf Hilferding, *Finance Capital* (Russian edition, Moscow, 1912). In spite of the mistake the author makes on the theory of money, and in spite of a certain inclination on his part to reconcile Marxism with opportunism, this work gives a very valuable theoretical analysis of 'the latest phase of capitalist development', as the subtitle runs. Indeed, what has been said of imperialism during the last few years, especially in an enormous number of magazine and newspaper articles, and also in the resolutions, for example, of the Chemnitz and Basle congresses which took

place in the autumn of 1912, has scarcely gone beyond the ideas expounded, or more exactly, summed up by the two writers mentioned above. . . .

Later on, I shall try to show briefly, and as simply as possible, the connection and relationships between the *principal* economic features of imperialism. I shall not be able to deal with the non-economic aspects of the question, however much they deserve to be dealt with. References to literature and other notes which, perhaps, would not interest all readers, are to be found at the end of this pamphlet.*

* In this edition, the author's notes are given as footnotes.

1

CONCENTRATION OF PRODUCTION AND MONOPOLIES

The enormous growth
of industry and the remarkably rapid concentration of production in ever-larger enterprises are one of the most characteristic features of capitalism. Modern production censuses give most complete and most exact data on this process.

In Germany, for example, out of every 1,000 industrial enterprises, large enterprises, i.e., those employing more than 50 workers, numbered three in 1882, six in 1895 and nine in 1907; and out of every 100 workers employed, this group of enterprises employed 22, 30 and 37, respectively. Concentration of production, however, is much more intense than the concentration of workers, since labour in the large enterprises is much more productive. This is shown by the figures on steam-engines and electric motors. If we take what in Germany is called industry in the broad sense of the term, that is, including commerce, transport, etc., we get the following picture. Large-scale enterprises, 30,588 out of a total of 3,265,623, that is to say, 0.9 per cent. These enterprises employ 5,700,000 workers out of a total of 14,400,000, i.e., 39.4 per cent; they use 6,600,000 steam horse power out of a total of 8,800,000, i.e., 75.3 per cent, and 1,200,000 kilowatts of electricity out of a total of 1,500,000, i.e., 77.2 per cent.

Less than one-hundredth of the total number of enterprises utilize *more than three-fourths* of the total amount of steam and electric power! Two million nine hundred and seventy thousand small enterprises (employing up to five workers), constituting 91 per cent of the total, utilize only 7 per cent of the total amount of steam and electric power! Tens of thousands of huge enterprises are everything; millions of small ones are nothing.

In 1907, there were in Germany 586 establishments employing one thousand and more workers, nearly *one-tenth* (1,380,000) of the total number of workers employed in industry, and they consumed *almost one-third* (32 per cent) of the total amount of steam and electric power.[1] As we shall see, money capital and the banks make this superiority of a handful of the largest enterprises still more overwhelming, in the most literal sense of the word, i.e., millions of small, medium and even some big 'proprietors' are in fact in complete subjection to some hundreds of millionaire financiers.

In another advanced country of modern capitalism, the United States of America, the growth of the concentration of production is still greater. Here statistics single out industry in the narrow sense of the word and classify enterprises according to the value of their annual output. In 1904 large-scale enterprises with an output valued at one million dollars and over numbered 1,900 (out of 216,180, i.e., 0.9 per cent). These employed 1,400,000 workers (out of 5,500,000, i.e., 25.6 per cent) and the value of their output amounted to $5,600,000,000 (out of $14,800,000,000, i.e., 38 per cent). Five years later, in 1909, the corresponding figures were: 3,060 enterprises (out of 268,491, i.e., 1.1 per cent) employing 2,000,000 workers (out of 6,600,000, i.e., 30.5 per cent) with an output valued at $9,000,000,000 (out of $20,700,000,000, i.e., 43.8 per cent).[2]

Almost half the total production of all the enterprises of the country was carried on by *one-hundredth part* of these enterprises! These 3,000 giant enterprises embrace 258 branches of industry. From this it can be seen that at a certain stage of its development concentration itself, as it were, leads straight to monopoly, for a score or so of giant enterprises can easily arrive at an agreement, and on the other hand, the hindrance to

[1] Figures taken from *Annalen des deutschen Reichs,* 1911, Zahn.
[2] *Statistical Abstract of the United States 1912,* p. 202.

competition, the tendency towards monopoly, arises from the huge size of the enterprises. This transformation of competition into monopoly is one of the most important – if not the most important – phenomena of modern capitalist economy, and we must deal with it in greater detail. But first we must clear up one possible misunderstanding.

American statistics speak of 3,000 giant enterprises in 250 branches of industry, as if there were only a dozen enterprises of the largest scale for each branch of industry.

But this is not the case. Not in every branch of industry are there large-scale enterprises; and moreover, a very important feature of capitalism in its highest stage of development is so-called *combination* of production, that is to say, the grouping in a single enterprise of different branches of industry, which either represent the consecutive stages in the processing of raw materials (for example, the smelting of iron ore into pig-iron, the conversion of pig-iron into steel, and then, perhaps, the manufacture of steel goods) – or are auxiliary to one another (for example, the utilization of scrap, or of by-products, the manufacture of packing materials, etc.).

'Combination,' writes Hilferding, 'levels out the fluctuations of trade and therefore assures to the combined enterprises a more stable rate of profit. Secondly, combination has the effect of eliminating trade. Thirdly, it has the effect of rendering possible technical improvements, and, consequently, the acquisition of superprofits over and above those obtained by the "pure" [i.e., non-combined] enterprises. Fourthly, it strengthens the position of the combined enterprises relative to the "pure" enterprises, strengthens them in the competitive struggle in periods of serious depression, when the fall in prices of raw materials does not keep pace with the fall in prices of manufactured goods.'[3]

The German bourgeois economist, Heymann, who has written a book especially on 'mixed', that is, combined, enterprises in the German iron industry, says: 'Pure enterprises perish, they are crushed between the high price of raw material and the low price of the finished product.' Thus we get the following picture: 'There remain, on the one hand, the big coal companies, producing millions of tons yearly, strongly organized in their coal syndicate, and on the other, the big steel plants, closely allied to the coal mines, having their own steel syndicate. These giant enterprises,

---

[3] *Finance Capital*, Russ. ed., pp. 286–87.

producing 400,000 tons of steel per annum, with a tremendous output of ore and coal and producing finished steel goods, employing 10,000 workers quartered in company houses, and sometimes owning their own railways and ports, are the typical representatives of the German iron and steel industry. And concentration goes on further and further. Individual enterprises are becoming larger and larger. An ever-increasing number of enterprises in one, or in several different industries, join together in giant enterprises, backed up and directed by half a dozen big Berlin banks. In relation to the German mining industry, the truth of the teachings of Karl Marx on concentration is definitely proved; true, this applies to a country where industry is protected by tariffs and freight rates. The German mining industry is ripe for expropriation.'[4]

Such is the conclusion which a bourgeois economist who, by way of exception, is conscientious, had to arrive at. It must be noted that he seems to place Germany in a special category because her industries are protected by higher tariffs. But this is a circumstance which only accelerates concentration and the formation of monopolist manufacturers' associations, cartels, syndicates, etc. It is extremely important to note that in free-trade Britain, concentration *also* leads to monopoly, although somewhat later and perhaps in another form. Professor Hermann Levy, in his special work of research entitled *Monopolies, Cartels and Trusts*, based on data on British economic development, writes as follows:

'In Great Britain it is the size of the enterprise and its high technical level which harbour a monopolist tendency. This, for one thing, is due to the great investment of capital per enterprise, which gives rise to increasing demands for new capital for the new enterprises and thereby renders their launching more difficult. Moreover (and this seems to us to be the more important point), every new enterprise that wants to keep pace with the gigantic enterprises that have been formed by concentration would here produce such an enormous quantity of surplus goods that it could dispose of them only by being able to sell them profitably as a result of an enormous increase in demand; otherwise, this surplus would force prices down to a level that would be unprofitable both for the new enterprise and for the monopoly combines.' Britain differs from other countries where protective

---

[4] Hans Gideon Heymann, *Die gemischten Werke im deutschen Grosseisen-gewerbe*, Stuttgart, 1904, S. 256, 278.

tariffs facilitate the formation of cartels in that monopolist manufacturers' associations, cartels and trusts arise in the majority of cases only when the number of the chief competing enterprises has been reduced to 'a couple of dozen or so'. 'Here the influence of concentration on the formation of large industrial monopolies in a whole sphere of industry stands out with crystal clarity.'[5]

Half a century ago, when Marx was writing *Capital*, free competition appeared to the overwhelming majority of economists to be a 'natural law'. Official science tried, by a conspiracy of silence, to kill the works of Marx, who by a theoretical and historical analysis of capitalism had proved that free competition gives rise to the concentration of production, which, in turn, at a certain stage of development, leads to monopoly. Today, monopoly has become a fact. Economists are writing mountains of books in which they describe the diverse manifestations of monopoly, and continue to declare in chorus that 'Marxism is refuted'. But facts are stubborn things, as the English proverb says, and they have to be reckoned with, whether we like it or not. The facts show that differences between capitalist countries, e.g., in the matter of protection or free trade, only give rise to insignificant variations in the form of monopolies or in the moment of their appearance; and that the rise of monopolies, as the result of the concentration of production, is a general and fundamental law of the present stage of development of capitalism.

For Europe, the time when the new capitalism *definitely* superseded the old can be established with fair precision; it was the beginning of the twentieth century. In one of the latest compilations on the history of the 'formation of monopolies', we read:

'Isolated examples of capitalist monopoly could be cited from the period preceding 1860; in these could be discerned the embryo of the forms that are so common today; but all this undoubtedly represents the prehistory of the cartels. The real beginning of modern monopoly goes back, at the earliest, to the sixties. The first important period of development of monopoly commenced with the international industrial depression of the seventies and lasted until the beginning of the nineties.' 'If we examine the question on a European scale, we will find that the development of free competition reached its apex in the sixties and seventies. It was then

---

[5] Hermann Levy, *Monopole, Kartelle und Trusts*, Jena, 1909, S. 286, 290, 298.

that Britain completed the construction of her old-style capitalist organization. In Germany, this organization had entered into a fierce struggle with handicraft and domestic industry, and had begun to create for itself its own forms of existence.'

'The great revolution commenced with the crash of 1873, or rather, the depression which followed it and which, with hardly discernible interruptions in the early eighties, and the unusually violent, but short-lived boom round about 1889, marks twenty-two years of European economic history.' 'During the short boom of 1889–90, the system of cartels was widely resorted to in order to take advantage of favourable business conditions. An ill-considered policy drove prices up still more rapidly and still higher than would have been the case if there had been no cartels, and nearly all these cartels perished ingloriously in the smash. Another five-year period of bad trade and low prices followed, but a new spirit reigned in industry; the depression was no longer regarded as something to be taken for granted; it was regarded as nothing more than a pause before another boom.

'The cartel movement entered its second epoch: instead of being a transitory phenomenon, the cartels have become one of the foundations of economic life. They are winning one field of industry after another, primarily, the raw materials industry. At the beginning of the nineties the cartel system had already acquired – in the organization of the coke syndicate on the model of which the coal syndicate was later formed – a cartel technique which has hardly been improved on. For the first time the great boom at the close of the nineteenth century and the crisis of 1900–03 occurred entirely – in the mining and iron industries at least – under the aegis of the cartels. And while at that time it appeared to be something novel, now the general public takes it for granted that large spheres of economic life have been, as a general rule, removed from the realm of free competition.'[6]

Thus, the principal stages in the history of monopolies are the following: (1) 1860–70, the highest stage, the apex of development of free competition; monopoly is in the barely discernible, embryonic stage.

---

[6] Th. Vogelstein, 'Die Finanzielle Organisation der kapitalistischen Industrie und die Monopolbildungen' in *Grundriss der Sozialokonomik*, VI. Abt., Tübingen, 1914. Cf., also by the same author: *Organisationsformen der Eisen-industrie und Textilindustrie in England und Amerika*, Bd. I, Lpz., 1910.

(2) After the crisis of 1873, a lengthy period of development of cartels; but they are still the exception. They are not yet durable. They are still a transitory phenomenon. (3) The boom at the end of the nineteenth century and the crisis of 1900–03. Cartels become one of the foundations of the whole of economic life. Capitalism has been transformed into imperialism.

Cartels come to an agreement on the terms of sale, dates of payment, etc. They divide the markets among themselves. They fix the quantity of goods to be produced. They fix prices. They divide the profits among the various enterprises, etc.

The number of cartels in Germany was estimated at about 250 in 1896 and at 385 in 1905, with about 12,000 firms participating.[7] But it is generally recognized that these figures are underestimations. From the statistics of German industry for 1907 we quoted above, it is evident that even these 12,000 very big enterprises probably consume more than half the steam and electric power used in the country. In the United States of America, the number of trusts in 1900 was estimated at 185 and in 1907, 250. American statistics divide all industrial enterprises into those belonging to individuals, to private firms or to corporations. The latter in 1904 comprised 23.6 per cent, and in 1909, 25.9 per cent, i.e., more than one-fourth of the total industrial enterprises in the country. These employed in 1904, 70.6 per cent, and in 1909, 75.6 per cent, i.e., more than three-fourths of the total wage-earners. Their output at these two dates was valued at $10,900,000,000 and $16,300,000,000, i.e., 73.7 per cent and 79.0 per cent of the total, respectively.

At times cartels and trusts concentrate in their hands seven- or eight-tenths of the total output of a given branch of industry. The Rhine-Westphalian Coal Syndicate, at its foundation in 1893, concentrated 86.7 per cent of the total coal output of the area, and in 1910 it already concentrated 95.4 per cent.[8] The monopoly so created assures enormous profits, and leads to the formation of technical production units of formidable magnitude. The famous Standard Oil Company in the United

---

[7] Dr. Riesser, *Die deutschen Grossbanken und ihre Konzentration im Zusammenhange mit der Entwicklung der Gesamtwirtschaft in Deutschland*, 4. Aufl., 1912, S. 149; Robert Liefmann, *Kartelle und Trusts und die Weiterbildung, der volkswirtschaftlichen Organisation*, 2. Aufl., 1910, S. 25.

[8] Dr. Fritz Kestner, *Der Organisationszwang. Eine Untersuchung über die Kampfe zwischen Kartellen und Aussenseitern*, Berlin, 1912, S. 11.

States was founded in 1900: 'It has an authorized capital of $150,000,000. It issued $100,000,000 common and $106,000,000 preferred stock. From 1900 to 1907 the following dividends were paid on the latter: 48, 48, 45, 44, 36, 40, 40, 40 per cent in the respective years, i.e., in all, $367,000,000. From 1882 to 1907, out of total net profits amounting to $889,000,000, $606,000,000 were distributed in dividends, and the rest went to reserve capital.'[9] 'In 1907 the various works of the United States Steel Corporation employed no less than 210,180 people. The largest enterprise in the German mining industry, Gelsenkirchener Bergwerksgesellschaft, in 1908 had a staff of 46,048 workers and office employees.'[10] In 1902, the United States Steel Corporation already produced 9,000,000 tons of steel.[11] Its output constituted in 1901, 66.3 per cent, and in 1908, 56.1 per cent of the total output of steel in the United States.[12] The output of ore was 43.9 per cent and 46.3 per cent, respectively.

The report of the American Government Commission on Trusts states: 'Their superiority over competitors is due to the magnitude of their enterprises and their excellent technical equipment. Since its inception, the Tobacco Trust has devoted all its efforts to the universal substitution of mechanical for manual labour. With this end in view it has bought up all patents that have anything to do with the manufacture of tobacco and has spent enormous sums for this purpose. Many of these patents at first proved to be of no use, and had to be modified by the engineers employed by the trust. At the end of 1906, two subsidiary companies were formed solely to acquire patents. With the same object in view, the trust has built its own foundries, machine shops and repair shops. One of these establishments, that in Brooklyn, employs on the average 300 workers; here experiments are carried out on inventions concerning the manufacture of cigarettes, cheroots, snuff, tinfoil for packing, boxes, etc. Here, also, inventions are perfected.'[13] 'Other trusts also employ what are called development engineers whose business it is to devise new methods of

---

[9] R. Liefmann, *Beteiligungs- und Finanzierungsgesellschaften. Eine Studie über den modernen Kapitalismus und das Effektenwesen*, 1. Aufl., Jena, 1909, S. 212.

[10] Ibid., S. 218.

[11] Dr. S. Tschierschky, *Kartell und Trust*, Gottingen, 1903, S. 13.

[12] Th. Vogelstein, *Organisationsformen*, S. 275.

[13] *Report of the Commissioner of Corporations on the Tobacco Industry*, Washington, 1909, p. 266, cited according to Dr. Paul Tafel: *Die nordamerikanischen Trusts und ihre Wirkungen auf den Fortschritt der Technik*, Stuttgart, 1913, S. 48.

production and to test technical improvements. The United States Steel Corporation grants big bonuses to its workers and engineers for all inventions that raise technical efficiency, or reduce cost of production.'[14]

In German large-scale industry, e.g., in the chemical industry, which has developed so enormously during these last few decades, the promotion of technical improvement is organized in the same way. By 1908 the process of concentration of production had already given rise to two main 'groups' which, in their way, were also in the nature of monopolies. At first these groups constituted 'dual alliances' of two pairs of big factories, each having a capital of from twenty to twenty-one million marks – on the one hand, the former Meister Factory in Hochst and the Casella Factory in Frankfurt am Main; and on the other hand, the aniline and soda factory at Ludwigshafen and the former Bayer Factory at Elberfeld. Then, in 1905, one of these groups, and in 1908 the other group, each concluded an agreement with yet another big factory. The result was the formation of two 'triple alliances', each with a capital of from forty to fifty million marks. And these 'alliances' have already begun to 'approach' each other, to reach 'an understanding' about prices, etc.[15]

Competition becomes transformed into monopoly. The result is immense progress in the socialization of production. In particular, the process of technical invention and improvement becomes socialized.

This is something quite different from the old free competition between manufacturers, scattered and out of touch with one another, and producing for an unknown market. Concentration has reached the point at which it is possible to make an approximate estimate of all sources of raw materials (for example, the iron ore deposits) of a country and even, as we shall see, of several countries, or of the whole world. Not only are such estimates made, but these sources are captured by gigantic monopolist associations. An approximate estimate of the capacity of markets is also made, and the associations 'divide' them up amongst themselves by agreement. Skilled labour is monopolized, the best engineers are engaged; the means of transport are captured – railways in America, shipping

[14] Dr. P. Tafel, ibid., S. 49.
[15] Riesser, op. cit., third edition, p. 547 et seq. The newspapers (June 1916) report the formation of a new gigantic trust which combines the chemical industry of Germany.

companies in Europe and America. Capitalism in its imperialist stage leads directly to the most comprehensive socialization of production; it, so to speak, drags the capitalists, against their will and consciousness, into some sort of a new social order, a transitional one from complete free competition to complete socialization.

Production becomes social, but appropriation remains private. The social means of production remain the private property of a few. The general framework of formally recognized free competition remains, and the yoke of a few monopolists on the rest of the population becomes a hundred times heavier, more burdensome and intolerable.

The German economist, Kestner, has written a book especially devoted to 'the struggle between the cartels and outsiders', i.e., the capitalists outside the cartels. He entitled his work *Compulsory Organization*, although, in order to present capitalism in its true light, he should, of course, have written about compulsory submission to monopolist associations. It is instructive to glance at least at the list of the methods the monopolist associations resort to in the present-day, the latest, the civilized struggle for 'organization': (1) stopping supplies of raw materials (. . . 'one of the most important methods of compelling adherence to the cartel'); (2) stopping the supply of labour by means of 'alliances' (i.e., of agreements between the capitalists and the trade unions by which the latter permit their members to work only in cartelized enterprises); (3) stopping deliveries; (4) closing trade outlets; (5) agreements with the buyers, by which the latter undertake to trade only with the cartels; (6) systematic price cutting (to ruin 'outside' firms, i.e., those which refuse to submit to the monopolists. Millions are spent in order to sell goods for a certain time below their cost price; there were instances when the price of petrol was thus reduced from 40 to 22 marks, i.e., almost by half!); (7) stopping credits; (8) boycott.

Here we no longer have competition between small and large, between technically developed and backward enterprises. We see here the monopolists throttling those who do not submit to them, to their yoke, to their dictation. This is how this process is reflected in the mind of a bourgeois economist:

'Even in the purely economic sphere,' writes Kestner, 'a certain change is taking place from commercial activity in the old sense of the word towards organizational-speculative activity. The greatest success no longer goes to the merchant whose technical and commercial experience enables him best of all to estimate the needs of the buyer, and who is able to discover and, so to speak, "awaken" a latent demand; it goes to the speculative genius [?!] who knows how to estimate, or even only to sense in advance, the organizational development and the possibilities of certain connections between individual enterprises and the banks. . . .'

Translated into ordinary human language this means that the development of capitalism has arrived at a stage when, although commodity production still 'reigns' and continues to be regarded as the basis of economic life, it has in reality been undermined and the bulk of the profits go to the 'geniuses' of financial manipulation. At the basis of these manipulations and swindles lies socialized production; but the immense progress of mankind, with achieved this socialization, goes to benefit . . . the speculators. We shall see later how 'on these grounds' reactionary, petty-bourgeois critics of capitalist imperialism dream of going *back* to 'free', 'peaceful', and 'honest' competition.

'The prolonged raising of prices which results from the formation of cartels,' says Kestner, 'has hitherto been observed only in respect of the most important means of production, particularly coal, iron and potassium, but never in respect of manufactured goods. Similarly, the increase in profits resulting from this raising of prices has been limited only to the industries which produce means of production. To this observation we must add that the industries which process raw materials (and not semi-manufactures) not only secure advantages from the cartel formation in the shape of high profits, to the detriment of the finished goods industry, but have also secured a *dominating position* over the latter, which did not exist under free competition.'[16]

The words which I have italicized reveal the essence of the case which the bourgeois economists admit so reluctantly and so rarely, and which the present-day defenders of opportunism, led by Kautsky, so zealously try to evade and brush aside. Domination, and the violence that is associated with it, such are the relationships that are typical of the 'latest phase of capitalist development'; this is what inevitably had to result, and has resulted, from the formation of all-powerful economic monopolies.

I shall give one more example of the methods employed by the

[16] Kestner, op. cit., S. 254.

cartels. Where it is possible to capture all or the chief sources of raw materials, the rise of cartels and formation of monopolies is particularly easy. It would be wrong, however, to assume that monopolies do not arise in other industries in which it is impossible to corner the sources of raw materials. The cement industry, for instance, can find its raw materials everywhere. Yet in Germany this industry too is strongly cartelized. The cement manufacturers have formed regional syndicates: South German, Rhine-Westphalian, etc. The prices fixed are monopoly prices: 230 to 280 marks a car-load, when the cost price is 180 marks! The enterprises pay a dividend of from 12 to 16 per cent – and it must not be forgotten that the 'geniuses' of modern speculation know how to pocket big profits besides what they draw in dividends. In order to prevent competition in such a profitable industry, the monopolists even resort to various stratagems: they spread false rumours about the bad situation in their industry; anonymous warnings are published in the newspapers, like the following:

'Capitalists, don't invest your capital in the cement industry!'; lastly, they buy up 'outsiders' (those outside the syndicates) and pay them compensation of 60,000, 80,000 and even 150,000 marks.[17] Monopoly hews a path for itself everywhere without scruple as to the means, from paying a 'modest' sum to buy off competitors, to the American device of employing dynamite against them.

The statement that cartels can abolish crises is a fable spread by bourgeois economists who at all costs desire to place capitalism in a favourable light. On the contrary, the monopoly created in *certain* branches of industry increases and intensifies the anarchy inherent in capitalist production *as a whole*. The disparity between the development of agriculture and that of industry, which is characteristic of capitalism in general, is increased. The privileged position of the most highly cartelized, so-called *heavy* industry, especially coal and iron, causes 'a still greater lack of co-ordination' in other branches of industry – as Jeidels, the author of one of the best works on 'the relationship of the German big banks to industry', admits.[18]

---

[17] L. Eschwege, 'Zement' in *Die Bank*, 1909, 1, S. 115 et seq.
[18] Jeidels, *Das Verhältnis der deutschen Grossbanken zur Industrie mit besonderer Berücksichtigung der Eisenindustrie*, Leipzig, 1905, S. 271.

'The more developed an economic system is,' writes Liefmann, an unblushing apologist of capitalism, 'the more it resorts to risky enterprises, or enterprises in other countries, to those which need a great deal of time to develop, or finally, to those which are only of local importance.'[19] The increased risk is connected in the long run with a prodigious increase of capital, which, as it were, overflows the brim, flows abroad, etc. At the same time the extremely rapid rate of technical progress gives rise to increasing elements of disparity between the various spheres of national economy, to anarchy and crises. Liefmann is obliged to admit that: 'In all probability mankind will see further important technical revolutions in the near future which will also affect the organization of the economic system' . . . electricity and aviation. . . . 'As a general rule, in such periods of radical economic change, speculation develops on a large scale.'. . .[20]

Crises of every kind – economic crises most frequently, but not only these – in their turn increase very considerably the tendency towards concentration and towards monopoly. In this connection, the following reflections of Jeidels on the significance of the crisis of 1900, which, as we have already seen, marked the turning-point in the history of modern monopoly, are exceedingly instructive: 'Side by side with the gigantic plants in the basic industries, the crisis of 1900 still found many plants organized on lines that today would be considered obsolete, the 'pure' (non-combined) plants, which were brought into being at the height of the industrial boom. The fall in prices and the falling off in demand put these 'pure' enterprises in a precarious position, which did not affect the gigantic combined enterprises at all or only affected them for a very short time. As a consequence of this the crisis of 1900 resulted in a far greater concentration of industry than the crisis of 1873: the latter crisis also produced a sort of selection of the best-equipped enterprises, but owing to the level of technical development at that time, this selection could not place the firms which successfully emerged from the crisis in a position of monopoly. Such a durable monopoly exists to a high degree in the gigantic enterprises in the modern iron and steel and electrical industries owing to their very complicated technique, far-reaching organization and magnitude of capital,

[19] Liefmann, *Beteilieungs- und Finanzierunesgesellschaften*, S. 434.
[20] Ibid., S. 465–66.

and, to a lesser degree, in the engineering industry, certain branches of the metallurgical industry, transport, etc.'[21]

Monopoly! This is the last word in the 'latest phase of capitalist development'. But we shall only have a very insufficient, incomplete, and poor notion of the real power and the significance of modern monopolies if we do not take into consideration the part played by the banks.

[21] Jeidels, op.cit., S. 108.

2

BANKS
AND THEIR NEW ROLE

The principal and
primary function of banks is to serve as middlemen in the making of
payments. In so doing they transform inactive money capital into active,
that is, into capital yielding a profit; they collect all kinds of money revenues
and place them at the disposal of the capitalist class.

As banking develops and becomes concentrated in a small number
of establishments, the banks grow from modest middlemen into powerful
monopolies having at their command almost the whole of the money
capital of all the capitalists and small businessmen and also the larger part
of the means of production and sources of raw materials in any one country
and in a number of countries. This transformation of numerous modest
middlemen into a handful of monopolists is one of the fundamental
processes in the growth of capitalism into capitalist imperialism; for this
reason we must first of all examine the concentration of banking.

In 1907–08, the combined deposits of the German joint-stock
banks, each having a capital of more than a million marks, amounted to
7,000 million marks; in 1912–13, these deposits already amounted to 9,800
million marks, an increase of 40 per cent in five years; and of the 2,800
million increase, 2,750 million was divided among 57 banks, each having

a capital of more than 10 million marks. The distribution of the deposits between big and small banks was as follows:[1]

PERCENTAGE OF TOTAL DEPOSITS

	In 9 big Berlin banks	In the other 48 banks with a capital of more than 10 million marks	In 115 banks with a capital of 1–10 million marks	In small banks (with a capital of less than a million marks)
1907–08	47	32.5	16.5	4
1912–13	49	36	12	3

The small banks are being squeezed out by the big banks, of which only nine concentrate in their hands almost half the total deposits. But we have left out of account many important details, for instance, the transformation of numerous small banks into actual branches of the big banks, etc. Of this I shall speak later on.

At the end of 1913, Schulze-Gaevernitz estimated the deposits in the nine big Berlin banks at 5,100 million marks, out of a total of about 10,000 million marks. Taking into account not only the deposits, but the total bank capital, this author wrote:

'At the end of 1909, the nine big Berlin banks, *together with their affiliated banks,* controlled 11,300 million marks, that is, about 83 per cent of the total German bank capital. The Deutsche Bank, which *together with its affiliated banks* controls nearly 3,000 million marks, represents, parallel to the Prussian State Railway Administration, the biggest and also the most decentralized accumulation of capital in the Old World.'[2]

I have emphasized the reference to the 'affiliated' banks because it is one of the most important distinguishing features of modern capitalist concentration. The big enterprises, and the banks in particular, not only completely absorb the small ones, but also 'annex' them, subordinate them, bring them into their 'own' group or 'concern' (to use the technical term) by acquiring 'holdings' in their capital, by purchasing or exchanging shares, by a system of credits, etc., etc. Professor Liefmann has written a volum-inous 'work' of about 500 pages describing modern 'holding and finance

[1] Alfred Lansburgh, 'Fünf Jahre deutsches Bankwesen' in *Die Bank*, 1913, No: 8, S. 728.
[2] Schulze-Gaevernitz, 'Die deutsche Kreditbank' in *Grundriss der Sozialökonomik*, Tübingen, 1915, S. 12, 137.

companies',[3] unfortunately adding very dubious 'theoretical' reflections to what is frequently undigested raw material. To what results this 'holding' system leads in respect of concentration is best illustrated in the book written on the big German banks by Riesser, himself a banker. But before examining his data, let us quote a concrete example of the 'holding' system.

The Deutsche Bank 'group' is one of the biggest, if not the biggest, of the big banking groups. In order to trace the main threads which connect all the banks in this group, a distinction must be made between holdings of the first and second and third degree, or what amounts to the same thing, between dependence (of the lesser banks on the Deutsche Bank) in the first, second and third degree. We then obtain the following picture:[4]

		Direct or 1st degree dependence	2nd degree dependence	3rd degree dependence
The Deutsche Bank has holdings	*Permanently*	in 17 other banks	9 of the 17 have holdings in 34 other banks	4 of the 9 have holdings in 7 other banks
	For an indefinite period	in 5 other banks	–	–
	Occasionally	in 8 other banks	5 of the 8 have holdings in 14 other banks	2 of the 5 have holdings in 2 other banks
	Total	in 30 other banks	14 of the 30 have holdings in 48 other banks	6 of the 14 have holdings in 9 other banks

Included in the eight banks 'occasionally' dependent on the Deutsche Bank in the 'first degree', are three foreign banks: one Austrian (the Wiener Bankverein) and two Russian (the Siberian Commercial Bank and the Russian Bank for Foreign Trade). Altogether, the Deutsche Bank group comprises, directly and indirectly, partially and totally, 87 banks; and the total capital – its own and that of others which it controls – is estimated at between two and three thousand million marks.

---

[3] R. Liefmann, *Beteiligungs- und Finanzierungsgesellschaften, Eine Studie über den modernen Kapitalismus und das Effektenwesen*, 1. Aufl., Jena, 1909. S. 212.

[4] Alfred Lansburgh, 'Das Beteiligungssystem im deutschen Bankwesen' in *Die Bank*, 1910, 1, S. 500.

It is obvious that a bank which stands at the head of such a group, and which enters into agreement with half a dozen other banks only slightly smaller than itself for the purpose of conducting exceptionally big and profitable financial operations like floating state loans, has already outgrown the part of 'middleman' and has become an association of a handful of monopolists.

The rapidity with which the concentration of banking proceeded in Germany at the turn of the twentieth century is shown by the following data which we quote in an abbreviated form from Riesser:

SIX BIG BERLIN BANKS

Year	Branches in Germany	Deposit banks and exchange offices	Constant holdings in German joint-stock banks	Total establishments
1895	16	14	1	42
1900	21	40	8	80
1911	104	276	63	450

We see the rapid expansion of a close network of channels which cover the whole country, centralizing all capital and all revenues, transforming thousands and thousands of scattered economic enterprises into a single national capitalist, and then into a world capitalist economy. The 'decentralization' that Schulze-Gaevernitz, as an exponent of present-day bourgeois political economy, speaks of in the passage previously quoted, really means the subordination to a single centre of an increasing number of formerly relatively 'independent', or rather, strictly local economic units. In reality it is *centralization*, the enhancement of the role, importance and power of monopolist giants.

In the older capitalist countries this 'banking network' is still more close. In Great Britain and Ireland, in 1910, there were in all 7,151 branches of banks. Four big banks had more than 400 branches each (from 447 to 689); four had more than 200 branches each, and eleven more than 100 each.

In France, *three* very big banks, Crédit Lyonnais, the Comptoir National and the Société Générale, extended their operations and their network of branches in the following manner.[5]

---

[5] Eugen Kaufmann, *Das französische Bankwesen*, Tübingen, 1911, S. 356 und 362.

	Number of branches and offices			Capital (*000,000 francs*)	
	In the provinces	In Paris	Total	Own capital	Deposits used as capital
1870	47	17	64	200	427
1890	192	66	258	265	1,245
1909	1,033	196	1,229	887	4,363

In order to show the 'connections' of a big modern bank, Riesser gives the following figures of the number of letters dispatched and received by the Disconto-Gesellschaft, one of the biggest banks in Germany and in the world (its capital in 1914 amounted to 300 million marks):

	Letters received	Letters dispatched
1852	6,135	6,292
1870	85,800	87,513
1900	533,102	161,043

The number of accounts of the big Paris bank, the Credit Lyonnais, increased from 28,535 in 1875 to 633,539 in 1912.[6]

These simple figures show perhaps better than lengthy disquisitions how the concentration of capital and the growth of bank turnover are radically changing the significance of the banks. Scattered capitalists are transformed into a single collective capitalist. When carrying the current accounts of a few capitalists, a bank, as it were, transacts a purely technical and exclusively auxiliary operation. When, however, this operation grows to enormous dimensions we find that a handful of monopolists subordinate to their will all the operations, both commercial and industrial, of the whole of capitalist society; for they are enabled – by means of their banking connections, their current accounts and other financial operations – first, to *ascertain exactly* the financial position of the various capitalists, then to *control* them, to influence them by restricting or enlarging, facilitating or hindering credits, and finally to *entirely determine* their fate, determine their income, deprive them of capital, or permit them to increase their capital rapidly and to enormous dimensions, etc.

---

[6] Jean Lescure, *L'epargne en France*, Paris, 1914, p. 52.

We have just mentioned the 300 million marks capital of the Disconto-Gesellschaft of Berlin. This increase of the capital of the bank was one of the incidents in the struggle for hegemony between two of the biggest Berlin banks – the Deutsche Bank and the Disconto. In 1870, the first was still a novice and had a capital of only 15 million marks, while the second had a capital of 30 million marks. In 1908, the first had a capital of 200 million, while the second had 170 million. In 1914, the first increased its capital to 250 million and the second, by merging with another first-class big bank, the Schaaffhausenscher Bankverein, increased its capital to 300 million. And, of course, this struggle for hegemony went hand in hand with the more and more frequent conclusion of 'agreements' of an increasingly durable character between the two banks. The following are the conclusions that this development forces upon banking specialists who regard economic questions from a standpoint which does not in the least exceed the bounds of the most moderate and cautious bourgeois reformism.

Commenting on the increase of the capital of the Disconto-Gesellschaft to 300 million marks, the German review, *Die Bank*, wrote: 'Other banks will follow this same path and in time the three hundred men, who today govern Germany economically, will gradually be reduced to fifty, twenty-five or still fewer. It cannot be expected that this latest move towards concentration will be confined to banking. The close relations that exist between individual banks naturally lead to the bringing together of the industrial syndicates which these banks favour. . . . One fine morning we shall wake up in surprise to see nothing but trusts before our eyes, and to find ourselves faced with the necessity of substituting state monopolies for private monopolies. However, we have nothing to reproach ourselves with, except that we have allowed things to follow their own course, slightly accelerated by the manipulation of stocks.'[7]

This is an example of the impotence of bourgeois journalism which differs from bourgeois science only in that the latter is less sincere and strives to obscure the essence of the matter, to hide the forest behind the trees. To be 'surprised' at the results of concentration, to 'reproach' the government of capitalist Germany, or capitalist 'society' ('ourselves'), to fear that the introduction of stocks and shares might 'accelerate'

---

[7]   A. Lansburgh, 'Die Bank mit den 300 Millionen' in *Die Bank*, 1914, 1, S. 426.

concentration in the same way as the German 'cartel' specialist Tschierschky fears the American trusts and 'prefers' the German cartels on the grounds that they 'may not, like the trusts, excessively accelerate technical and economic progress[8] – is not all this a sign of impotence?

But facts remain facts. There are no trusts in Germany; there are 'only' cartels – but Germany is *governed* by not more than three hundred magnates of capital, and the number of these is constantly diminishing. At all events, banks greatly intensify and accelerate the process of concentration of capital and the formation of monopolies in all capitalist countries, notwithstanding all the differences in their banking laws.

The banking system 'possesses, indeed, the form of universal book-keeping and distribution of means of production on a social scale, but solely the form', wrote Marx in *Capital* half a century ago (Russ. trans., Vol. III, part II, p. 144 [*Capital*, Vol. III, Moscow: Progress Publishers, 1971, p. 606]). The figures we have quoted on the growth of bank capital, on the increase in the number of the branches and offices of the biggest banks, the increase in the number of their accounts, etc., present a concrete picture of this 'universal book-keeping' of the *whole* capitalist class; and not only of the capitalists, for the banks collect, even though temporarily, all kinds of money revenues – of small businessmen, office clerks, and of a tiny upper stratum of the working class. 'Universal distribution of means of production' – that, from the formal aspect, is what *grows* out of the modern banks, which, numbering some three to six of the biggest in France, and six to eight in Germany, control millions and millions. In *substance*, however, the distribution of means of production is not at all 'universal', but private, i.e., it conforms to the interests of big capital, and primarily, of huge, monopoly capital, which operates under conditions in which the masses live in want, in which the whole development of agriculture hopelessly lags behind the development of industry, while within industry itself the 'heavy industries' exact tribute from all other branches of industry.

In the matter of socializing capitalist economy the savings-banks and post-offices are beginning to compete with the banks; they are more 'decentralized', i.e., their influence extends to a greater number of localities, to more remote places, to wider sections of the population. Here is the

[8] S. Tschierschky, op. cit., S. 128.

data collected by an American commission on the comparative growth of deposits in banks and savings-banks:[9]

DEPOSITS (*000,000,000 marks*)

	Britain		France		Germany		
	Banks	**Savings Banks**	**Banks**	**Savings banks**	**Banks**	**Credit societies**	**Savings banks**
1880	8.4	1.6	?	0.9	0.5	0.4	2.6
1888	12.4	2.0	1.5	2.1	1.1	0.4	4.5
1908	23.2	4.2	3.7	4.2	7.1	2.2	13.9

As they pay interest at the rate of 4 per cent and 4¼ per cent on deposits, the savings-banks must seek 'profitable' investments for their capital, they must deal in bills, mortgages, etc. The boundaries between the banks and the savings-banks 'become more and more obliterated'. The Chambers of Commerce of Bochum and Erfurt, for example, demand that savings-banks be 'prohibited' from engaging in 'purely' banking business, such as discounting bills; they demand the limitation of the 'banking' operations of the post-office.[10] The banking magnates seem to be afraid that state monopoly will steal upon them from an unexpected quarter. It goes without saying, however, that this fear is no more than an expression of the rivalry, so to speak, between two department managers in the same office; for, on the one hand, the millions entrusted to the savings-banks are in the final analysis actually controlled by *these very same* bank capital magnates, while, on the other hand, state monopoly in capitalist society is merely a means of increasing and guaranteeing the income of millionaires in some branch of industry who are on the verge of bankruptcy.

The change from the old type of capitalism, in which free competition predominated, to the new capitalism, in which monopoly reigns, is expressed, among other things, by a decline in the importance of the Stock Exchange. The review, *Die Bank*, writes:

'The Stock Exchange has long ceased to be the indispensable

---

[9] *Statistics of the National Monetary Commission,* quoted in *Die Bank* 1910, 2, S. 1200.
[10] *Die Bank,* 1913, S. 811, 1022; 1914; S. 713.

medium of circulation that it formerly was when the banks were not yet able to place the bulk of new issues with their clients.'[11]

'Every bank is a Stock Exchange', and the bigger the bank, and the more successful the concentration of banking, the truer does this modern aphorism ring.'[12] 'While formerly, in the seventies, the Stock Exchange, flushed with the exuberance of youth' [a 'subtle' allusion to the Stock Exchange crash of 1873, the company promotion scandals, etc.], 'opened the era of the industrialization of Germany, nowadays the banks and industry are able to "manage it alone". The domination of our big banks over the Stock Exchange . . . is nothing else than the expression of the completely organized German industrial state. If the domain of the automatically functioning economic laws is thus restricted, and if the domain of conscious regulation by the banks is considerably enlarged, the national economic responsibility of a few guiding heads is immensely increased,' so writes the German Professor Schulze-Gaevernitz,[13] an apologist of German imperialism, who is regarded as an authority by the imperialists of all countries, and who tries to gloss over the 'mere detail' that the 'conscious regulation' of economic life by the banks consists in the fleecing of the public by a handful of 'completely organized' monopolists. The task of a bourgeois professor is not to lay bare the entire mechanism, or to expose all the machinations of the bank monopolists, but rather to present them in a favourable light.

In the same way, Riesser, a still more authoritative economist and himself a banker, makes shift with meaningless phrases in order to explain away undeniable facts: '. . . the Stock Exchange is steadily losing the feature which is absolutely essential for national economy as a whole and for the circulation of securities in particular – that of being not only a most exact measuring-rod, but also an almost automatic regulator of the economic movements which converge on it.'[14]

In other words, the old capitalism, the capitalism of free competition with its indispensable regulator, the Stock Exchange, is passing

---

[11] *Die Bank*, 1914, 1, S. 316.

[12] Dr Oscar Stillich, *Geld- und Bankwesen*, Berlin, 1907, S. 169.

[13] Schulze-Gaevernitz, 'Die deutsche Kreditbank' in *Grundriss der Sozial-ökonomik*, Tübingen, 1915. S. 101.

[14] Riesser, op. cit, 4th ed., S. 629.

away. A new capitalism has come to take its place, bearing obvious features of something transient, a mixture of free competition and monopoly. The question naturally arises: *into what* is this new capitalism 'developing'? But the bourgeois scholars are afraid to raise this question.

'Thirty years ago, businessmen, freely competing against one another, performed nine-tenths of the work connected with their business other than manual labour. At the present time, nine-tenths of this 'brain work' is performed by *employees*. Banking is in the forefront of this evolution.'[15] This admission by Schulze-Gaevernitz brings us once again to the question: into what is this new capitalism, capitalism in its imperialist stage, developing?

Among the few banks which remain at the head of all capitalist economy as a result of the process of concentration, there is naturally to be observed an increasingly marked tendency towards monopolist agreements, towards a *bank trust*. In America, not nine, but *two* very big banks, those of the multimillionaires Rockefeller and Morgan, control a capital of eleven thousand million marks.[16] In Germany the absorption of the Schaaffhausenscher Bankverein by the Disconto-Gesellschaft to which I referred above, was commented on in the following terms by the *Frankfurter Zeitung*, an organ of Stock Exchange interests:

'The concentration movement of the banks is narrowing the circle of establishments from which it is possible to obtain credits, and is consequently increasing the dependence of big industry upon a small number of banking groups. In view of the close connection between industry and the financial world, the freedom of movement of industrial companies which need banking capital is restricted. For this reason, big industry is watching the growing trustification of the banks with mixed feelings. Indeed, we have repeatedly seen the beginnings of certain agreements between the individual big banking concerns, which aim at restricting competition.'[17]

Again and again, the final word in the development of banking is monopoly.

As regards the close connection between the banks and industry,

---

[15] Schulze-Gaevernitz, 'Die deutsche Kreditbank' in *Grundriss der Sozialökonomik*, Tübingen, 1915, S. 151.

[16] *Die Bank*, 1912, 1, S. 435.

[17] Quoted by Schulze-Gaevernitz, op. cit., S. 155.

it is precisely in this sphere that the new role of the banks is, perhaps, most strikingly felt. When a bank discounts a bill for a firm, opens a current account for it, etc., these operations, taken separately, do not in the least diminish its independence, and the bank plays no other part than that of a modest middleman. But when such operations are multiplied and become an established practice, when the bank 'collects' in its own hands enormous amounts of capital, when the running of a current account for a given firm enables the bank – and this is what happens – to obtain fuller and more detailed information about the economic position of its client, the result is that the industrial capitalist becomes more completely dependent on the bank.

At the same time a personal link-up, so to speak, is established between the banks and the biggest industrial and commercial enterprises, the merging of one with another through the acquisition of shares, through the appointment of bank directors to the Supervisory Boards (or Boards of Directors) of industrial and commercial enterprises, and vice versa. The German economist, Jeidels, has compiled most detailed data on this form of concentration of capital and of enterprises. Six of the biggest Berlin banks were represented by their directors in *344* industrial companies; and by their board members in *407* others, making a total of *751* companies. In *289* of these companies they either had two of their representatives on each of the respective Supervisory Boards, or held the posts of chairmen. We find these industrial and commercial companies in the most diverse branches of industry: insurance, transport, restaurants, theatres, art industry, etc. On the other hand, on the Supervisory Boards of these six banks (in 1910) were fifty-one of the biggest industrialists, including the director of Krupp, of the powerful 'Hapag' (Hamburg-Amerika Line), etc., etc. From 1895 to 1910, each of these six banks participated in the share and bond issues of many hundreds of industrial companies (the number ranging from 281 to 419).[18]

The 'personal link-up' between the banks and industry is supplemented by the 'personal link-up' between both of them and the government. 'Seats on Supervisory Boards,' writes Jeidels, 'are freely offered to persons of title, also to ex-civil servants, who are able to do a great deal

---

[18] Jeidels, op. cit.; Riesser, op. cit.

to facilitate [!!] relations with the authorities.' . . . 'Usually, on the Supervisory Board of a big bank, there is a member of parliament or a Berlin city councillor.'

The building and development, so to speak, of the big capitalist monopolies is therefore going on full steam ahead in all 'natural' and 'supernatural' ways. A sort of division of labour is being systematically developed among the several hundred kings of finance who reign over modern capitalist society:

'Simultaneously with this widening of the sphere of activity of certain big industrialists [joining the boards of banks, etc.] and with the assignment of provincial bank managers to definite industrial regions, there is a growth of specialization among the directors of the big banks. Generally speaking, this specialization is only conceivable when banking is conducted on a large scale, and particularly when it has widespread connections with industry. This division of labour proceeds along two lines: on the one hand, relations with industry as a whole are entrusted to one director, as his special function; on the other, each director assumes the supervision of several separate enterprises, or of a group of enterprises in the same branch of industry or having similar interests. . . . [Capitalism has already reached the stage of organized *supervision* of individual enterprises.] One specializes in German industry, sometimes even in West German industry alone [the West is the most industrialized part of Germany], others specialize in relations with foreign states and foreign industry, in information on the characters of industrialists and others, in Stock Exchange questions, etc. Besides, each bank director is often assigned a special locality or a special branch of industry; one works chiefly on Supervisory Boards of electric companies, another, on chemical, brewing, or beet sugar plants, a third, in a few isolated industrial enterprises, but at the same time works on the Supervisory Boards of insurance companies. . . . In short, there can be no doubt that the growth in the dimensions and diversity of the big banks' operations is accompanied by an increase in the division of labour among their directors with the object (and result) of, so to speak, lifting them somewhat out of pure banking and making them better experts, better judges of the general problems of industry and the special problems of each branch of industry, thus making them more capable of acting within the respective bank's industrial sphere of influence. This system is supplemented by the banks' endeavours to elect to their Supervisory Boards men who are experts in industrial affairs, such as industrialists, former officials, especially those formerly in the railway service or in mining,' etc.[19]

We find the same system only in a slightly different form in French banking. For instance, one of the three biggest French banks, the Crédit Lyonnais, has organized a financial research service (*service des etudes financières*), which permanently employs over fifty engineers, statisticians, economists, lawyers, etc. This costs from six to seven hundred thousand francs annually. The service is in turn divided into eight departments: one specializes in collecting information on industrial establishments, another studies general statistics, a third, railway and steamship companies, a fourth, securities, a fifth, financial reports, etc.[20]

The result is, on the one hand, the ever-growing merger, or, as N.I. Bukharin aptly calls it, coalescence, of bank and industrial capital and, on the other hand, the growth of the banks into institutions of a truly 'universal character'. On this question I find it necessary to quote the exact terms used by Jeidels, who has best studied the subject:

'An examination of the sum total of industrial relationships reveals the *universal character* of the financial establishments working on behalf of industry. Unlike other kinds of banks, and contrary to the demand sometimes expressed in the literature that banks should specialize in one kind of business or in one branch of industry in order to prevent the ground from slipping from under their feet – the big banks are striving to make their connections with industrial enterprises as varied as possible in respect of the locality or branches of industry and are striving to eliminate the unevenness in the distribution of capital among localities and branches of industry resulting from the historical development of individual enterprises.' 'One tendency is to make the connections with industry general; another tendency is to make them durable and close. In the six big banks both these tendencies are realized, not in full, but to a considerable extent and to an equal degree.'

Quite often industrial and commercial circles complain of the 'terrorism' of the banks. And it is not surprising that such complaints are heard, for the big banks 'command', as will be seen from the following example. On November 19, 1901, one of the big, so-called Berlin 'D' banks

---

[19] Jeidels, op. cit, S. 157.
[20] An article by Eug. Kaufmann on French banks in *Die Bank*, 1909, 2, S. 851 et seq.

(the names of the four biggest banks begin with the letter D) wrote to the Board of Directors of the German Central Northwest Cement Syndicate in the following terms: 'As we learn from the notice you published in a certain newspaper of the 18th inst., we must reckon with the possibility that the next general meeting of your syndicate, to be held on the 30th of this month, may decide on measures which are likely to effect changes in your enterprise which are unacceptable to us. We deeply regret that, for these reasons, we are obliged henceforth to withdraw the credit which had hitherto been allowed you. . . . But if the said next general meeting does not decide upon measures which are unacceptable to us, and if we receive suitable guarantees on this matter for the future, we shall be quite willing to open negotiations with you on the grant of a new credit.'[21]

As a matter of fact, this is small capital's old complaint about being oppressed by big capital, but in this case it was a whole syndicate that fell into the category of 'small' capital! The old struggle between small and big capital is being resumed at a new and immeasurably higher stage of development. It stands to reason that the big banks' enterprises, worth many millions, can accelerate technical progress with means that cannot possibly be compared with those of the past. The banks, for example, set up special technical research societies, and, of course, only 'friendly' industrial enterprises benefit from their work. To this category belong the Electric Railway Research Association, the Central Bureau of Scientific and Technical Research, etc.

The directors of the big banks themselves cannot fail to see that new conditions of national economy are being created; but they are powerless in the face of these phenomena.

'Anyone who has watched, in recent years,' writes Jeidels, 'the changes of incumbents of directorships and seats on the Supervisory Boards of the big banks, cannot fail to have noticed that power is gradually passing into the hands of men who consider the active intervention of the big banks in the general development of industry to be necessary and of increasing importance. Between these new men and the old bank directors, disagreements on this subject of a business and often of a personal nature are growing. The issue is whether or not the banks, as credit institutions, will suffer from this intervention in industry, whether they are sacrificing

---

[21] Dr Oscar Stillich, *Geld- und Bankwesen*, Berlin, 1907, S. 148.

tried principles and an assured profit to engage in a field of activity which has nothing in common with their role as middlemen in providing credit, and which is leading the banks into a field where they are more than ever before exposed to the blind forces of trade fluctuations. This is the opinion of many of the older bank directors, while most of the young men consider active intervention in industry to be a necessity as great as that which gave rise, simultaneously with big modern industry, to the big banks and modern industrial banking. The two parties are agreed only on one point: that there are neither firm principles nor a concrete aim in the new activities of the big banks.'[22]

The old capitalism has had its day. The new capitalism represents a transition towards something. It is hopeless, of course, to seek for 'firm principles and a concrete aim' for the purpose of 'reconciling' monopoly with free competition. The admission of the practical men has quite a different ring from the official praises of the charms of 'organized' capitalism sung by its apologists, Schulze-Gaevernitz, Liefmann and similar 'theoreticians'.

At precisely what period were the 'new activities' of the big banks finally established? Jeidels gives us a fairly exact answer to this important question:

'The connections between the banks and industrial enterprises, with their new content, their new forms and their new organs, namely, the big banks which are organized on both a centralized and a decentralized basis, were scarcely a characteristic economic phenomenon before the nineties; in one sense, indeed, this initial date may be advanced to the year 1897, when the important "mergers" took place and when, for the first time, the new form of decentralized organization was introduced to suit the industrial policy of the banks. This starting-point could perhaps be placed at an even later date, for it was the crisis of 1900 that enormously accelerated and intensified the process of concentration of industry and of banking, consolidated that process, for the first time transformed the connection with industry into the actual monopoly of the big banks, and made this connection much closer and more active.'[23]

[22] Jeidels, op. cit, S. 183–84.
[23] Ibid., S, 181.

Thus, the twentieth century marks the turning-point from the old capitalism to the new, from the domination of capital in general to the domination of finance capital.

3 FINANCE CAPITAL AND THE FINANCIAL OLIGARCHY

'A steadily increasing proportion of capital in industry,' writes Hilferding, 'ceases to belong to the industrialists who employ it. They obtain the use of it only through the medium of the banks which, in relation to them, represent the owners of the capital. On the other hand, the bank is forced to sink an increasing share of its funds in industry. Thus, to an ever greater degree the banker is being transformed into an industrial capitalist. This bank capital, i.e., capital in money form, which is thus actually transformed into industrial capital, I call "finance capital".' 'Finance capital is capital controlled by banks and employed by industrialists.'[1]

This definition is incomplete insofar as it is silent on one extremely important fact – on the increase of concentration of production and of capital to such an extent that concentration is leading, and has led, to monopoly. But throughout the whole of his work, and particularly in the two chapters preceding the one from which this definition is taken, Hilferding stresses the part played by *capitalist monopolies*.

[1] R. Hilferding, *Finance Capital*, Moscow, 1912 (in Russian), pp. 338–39.

The concentration of production; the monopolies arising therefrom; the merging or coalescence of the banks with industry – such is the history of the rise of finance capital and such is the content of that concept.

We now have to describe how, under the general conditions of commodity production and private property, the 'business operations' of capitalist monopolies inevitably lead to the domination of a financial oligarchy. It should be noted that German – and not only German – bourgeois scholars, like Riesser, Schulze-Gaevernitz, Liefmann and others, are all apologists of imperialism and of finance capital. Instead of revealing the 'mechanics' of the formation of an oligarchy, its methods, the size of its revenues 'impeccable and peccable', its connections with parliaments, etc., etc., they obscure or gloss over them. They evade these 'vexed questions' by pompous and vague phrases, appeals to the 'sense of responsibility' of bank directors, by praising 'the sense of duty' of Prussian officials, giving serious study to the petty details of absolutely ridiculous parliamentary bills for the 'supervision' and 'regulation' of monopolies, playing spillikins with theories, like, for example, the following 'scholarly' definition, arrived at by Professor Liefmann: '*Commerce* is *an occupation having for its object the collection, storage and supply of goods*,'[2] (The Professor's bold-face italics.) . . . From this it would follow that commerce existed in the time of primitive man, who knew nothing about exchange, and that it will exist under socialism!

But the monstrous facts concerning the monstrous rule of the financial oligarchy are so glaring that in all capitalist countries, in America, France and Germany, a whole literature has sprung up, written from the *bourgeois* point of view, but which, nevertheless, gives a fairly truthful picture and criticism – petty-bourgeois, naturally – of this oligarchy.

Paramount importance attaches to the 'holding system', already briefly referred to above. The German economist, Heymann, probably the first to call attention to this matter, describes the essence of it in this way:

'The head of the concern controls the principal company [literally: the 'mother company']; the latter reigns over the subsidiary companies ['daughter companies'] which in their turn control still other subsidiaries

---

[2] R. Liefmann, op. cit., S. 476.

['grandchild companies'], etc. In this way, it is possible with a comparatively small capital to dominate immense spheres of production. Indeed, if holding 50 per cent of the capital is always sufficient to control a company, the head of the concern needs only one million to control eight million in the second subsidiaries. And if this 'interlocking' is extended, it is possible with one million to control sixteen million, thirty-two million, etc.'[3]

As a matter of fact, experience shows that it is sufficient to own 40 per cent of the shares of a company in order to direct its affairs,[4] since in practice a certain number of small, scattered shareholders find it impossible to attend general meetings, etc. The 'democratization' of the ownership of shares, from which the bourgeois sophists and opportunist so-called 'Social-Democrats' expect (or say that they expect) the 'democratization of capital', the strengthening of the role and significance of small-scale production, etc., is, in fact, one of the ways of increasing the power of the financial oligarchy. Incidentally, this is why, in the more advanced, or in the older and more 'experienced' capitalist countries, the law allows the issue of shares of smaller denomination. In Germany, the law does not permit the issue of shares of less than one thousand marks denomination, and the magnates of German finance look with an envious eye at Britain, where the issue of one-pound shares (=20 marks, about 10 rubles) is permitted. Siemens, one of the biggest industrialists and 'financial kings' in Germany, told the Reichstag on June 7, 1900, that 'the one-pound share is the basis of British imperialism'.[5] This merchant has a much deeper and more 'Marxist' understanding of imperialism than a certain disreputable writer who is held to be one of the founders of Russian Marxism and believes that imperialism is a bad habit of a certain nation . . .

But the 'holding system' not only serves enormously to increase the power of the monopolists; it also enables them to resort with impunity to all sorts of shady and dirty tricks to cheat the public, because formally the directors of the 'mother company' are not legally responsible for the

[3] Hans Gideon Heymann, *Die gemischten Werke im deutschen Grosseisen-gewerbe*, Stuttgart, 1904, S. 268–69.

[4] Liefmann, *Beteiligungsgesellschaften*, etc., S. 258 of the first edition.

[5] Schulze-Gaevernitz in *Grundriss der Sozialökonomik*, V, 2, S. 110.

'daughter company', which is supposed to be 'independent', and *through the medium* of which they can 'pull off' *anything,* Here is an example taken from the German review, *Die Bank,* for May 1914:

'The Spring Steel Company of Kassel was regarded some years ago as being one of the most profitable enterprises in Germany. Through bad management its dividends fell from 15 per cent to nil. It appears that the Board, without consulting the shareholders, had loaned *six million marks* to one of its 'daughter companies', the Hassia Company, which had a nominal capital of only some hundreds of thousands of marks. This commitment, amounting to nearly treble the capital of the 'mother company', was never mentioned in its balance-sheets. This omission was quite legal and could be hushed up for two whole years because it did not violate any point of company law. The chairman of the Supervisory Board, who as the responsible head had signed the false balance-sheets, was, and still is, the president of the Kassel Chamber of Commerce. The shareholders only heard of the loan to the Hassia Company long afterwards, when it had been proved to be a mistake'. . . (the writer should put this word in inverted commas) . . . 'and when Spring Steel shares dropped nearly 100 per cent, because those in the know were getting rid of them. . . .

'*This typical example of balance-sheet jugglery, quite common* in joint-stock companies, explains why their Boards of Directors are willing to undertake risky transactions with a far lighter heart than individual businessmen. Modern methods of drawing up balance-sheets not only make it possible to conceal doubtful undertakings from the ordinary shareholder, but also allow the people most concerned to escape the consequence of unsuccessful speculation by selling their shares in time when the individual businessman risks his own skin in everything he does. . . .

'The balance-sheets of many joint-stock companies put us in mind of the palimpsests of the Middle Ages from which the visible inscription had first to be erased in order to discover beneath it another inscription giving the real meaning of the document. [Palimpsests are parchment documents from which the original inscription has been erased and another inscription imposed.]

'The simplest and, therefore, most common procedure for making balance-sheets indecipherable is to divide a single business into several parts by setting up 'daughter companies' – or by annexing them. The advantages of this system for various purposes – legal and illegal – are so evident that big companies which do not employ it are quite the exception.'[6]

As an example of a huge monopolist company that extensively employs this system, the author quotes the famous General Electric Company (the A.E.G., to which I shall refer again later on). In 1912, it was calculated that this company held shares in *175* to *200* other companies, dominating them, of course, and thus controlling a total capital of about *1,500 million marks.*[7]

None of the rules of control, the publication of balance-sheets, the drawing up of balance-sheets according to a definite form, the public auditing of accounts, etc., the things about which well-intentioned professors and officials – that is, those imbued with the good intention of defending and prettyfying capitalism – discourse to the public, are of any avail; for private property is sacred, and no one can be prohibited from buying, selling, exchanging or hypothecating shares, etc.

The extent to which this 'holding system' has developed in the big Russian banks may be judged by the figures given by E. Agahd, who for fifteen years was an official of the Russo–Chinese Bank and who, in May 1914, published a book, not altogether correctly entitled *Big Banks and the World Market.*[8] The author divides the big Russian banks into two main groups: (a) banks that come under the 'holding system', and (b) 'independent' banks – 'independence', however, being arbitrarily taken to mean independence of *foreign* banks. The author divides the first group into three subgroups: (1) German holdings, (2) British holdings, and (3) French holdings, having in view the 'holdings' and domination of the big foreign banks of the particular country mentioned. The author divides the capital of the banks into 'productively' invested capital (industrial and commercial undertakings), and 'speculatively' invested capital (in Stock Exchange and financial operations), assuming, from his petty-bourgeois reformist point of view, that it is possible, under capitalism, to separate the first form of investment from the second and to abolish the second form.

---

[6] L. Eschwege, 'Tochtergesellschaften' in *Die Bank*, 1914, 1, S. 545.

[7] Kurt Heinig, 'Der Weg des Elektrotrusts' in *Die Neue Zeit*, 1912, 30. Jahrg., 2, S. 484.

[8] E. Agahd, *Grossbanken und Weltmarkt, Die wirtschaftliche und politische Bedeutung der Grossbanken im Weltmarkt unter Berücksichtigung ihres Einflusses auf Russlands Volkswirtschaft und die deutsche-russischen Beziehungen*, Berlin, 1914.

Here are the figures he supplies:

BANK ASSETS (According to Reports for October–November 1913)
000,000 rubles

Groups of Russian banks	Capital invested		
	Productively	Speculatively	Total
a 1) *Four banks: Siberian Commercial, Russian, International, and Discount Bank*	413.7	859.1	1,272.8
a 2) *Two banks: Commercial and Industrial, and Russo-British*	239.3	169.1	408.4
a 3) *Five banks: Russian-Asiatic, St. Petersburg Private, Azov-Don, Union Moscow, Russo-French Commercial*	711.8	661.2	1,373.0
(*11 banks*) *Total* a)=	1,364.8	1,689.4	3,054.2
b) *Eight banks: Moscow Merchants, Volga-Kama, Junker and Co., St. Petersburg Commercial (formerly Wawelberg), Bank of Moscow (formerly Ryabushinsky), Moscow Discount, Moscow Commercial, Moscow Private*	504.2	391.1	895.3
(*19 banks*) *Total*	1,869.0	2,080.5	3,949.5

According to these figures, of the approximately 4,000 million rubles making up the 'working' capital of the big banks, *more than three-fourths*, more than 3,000 million, belonged to banks which in reality were only 'daughter companies' of foreign banks, and chiefly of Paris banks (the famous trio: Union Parisienne, Paris et Pays-Bas and Société Générale), and of Berlin banks (particularly the Deutsche Bank and Disconto-Gesellschaft). Two of the biggest Russian banks, the Russian (Russian Bank for Foreign Trade) and the International (St. Petersburg International Commercial Bank), between 1906 and 1912 increased their capital from 44 to 98 million rubles, and their reserves from 15 million to 39 million 'employing three-fourths German capital'. The first bank belongs to the Berlin Deutsche Bank 'concern' and the second to the Berlin Disconto-Gesellschaft. The worthy Agahd is deeply indignant at the majority of the shares being held by the Berlin banks, so that the Russian shareholders are, therefore, powerless. Naturally, the country which exports capital skims the cream; for example, the Berlin Deutsche Bank, before placing the shares of the Siberian Commercial Bank on the Berlin market, kept them in its portfolio for a whole year, and then sold them at the rate of 193 for 100, that is, at nearly twice their nominal value, 'earning' a profit of nearly six million rubles, which Hilferding calls 'promoter's profits'.

Our author puts the total 'capacity' of the principal St. Petersburg banks at 8,235 million rubles, well over 8,000 million, and the 'holdings', or rather, the extent to which foreign banks dominated them, he estimates as follows: French banks, 55 per cent; British, 10 per cent; German, 35 per cent. The author calculates that of the total of 8,235 million rubles of functioning capital, 3,687 million rubles, or over 40 per cent, fall to the share of the Produgol and Prodamet syndicates and the syndicates in the oil, metallurgical and cement industries. Thus, owing to the formation of capitalist monopolies, the merging of bank and industrial capital has also made enormous strides in Russia.

Finance capital, concentrated in a few hands and exercising a virtual monopoly, exacts enormous and ever-increasing profits from the floating of companies, issue of stock, state loans, etc., strengthens the domination of the financial oligarchy and levies tribute upon the whole of society for the benefit of monopolists. Here is an example, taken from a multitude of others, of the 'business' methods of the American trusts, quoted by Hilferding. In 1887, Havemeyer founded the Sugar Trust by amalgamating fifteen small firms, whose total capital amounted to 6,500,000 dollars. Suitably 'watered', as the Americans say, the capital of the trust was declared to be 50 million dollars. This 'overcapitalization' anticipated the monopoly profits, in the same way as the United States Steel Corporation anticipates its monopoly profits in buying up as many iron ore fields as possible. In fact, the Sugar Trust set up monopoly prices, which secured it such profits that it could pay 10 per cent dividend on capital 'watered' *sevenfold*, or *about 70 per cent on the capital actually invested at the time the trust was formed*! In 1909, the capital of the Sugar Trust amounted to 90 million dollars. In twenty-two years, it had increased its capital more than tenfold.

In France the domination of the 'financial oligarchy' (*Against the Financial Oligarchy in France*, the title of the well-known book by Lysis, the fifth edition of which was published in 1908) assumed a form that was only slightly different. Four of the most powerful banks enjoy, not a relative, but an 'absolute monopoly' in the issue of bonds. In reality, this is a 'trust of big banks'. And monopoly ensures monopoly profits from bond issues. Usually a borrowing country does not get more than 90 per cent of the sum of the loan, the remaining 10 per cent goes to the banks and other middlemen. The profit made by the banks out of the Russo–Chinese loan of 400 million francs amounted to 8 per cent; out of the Russian (1904) loan of 800 million francs the profit amounted to 10 per cent; and out of the Moroccan (1904) loan of 62,500,000 francs it amounted to 18.75 per cent. Capitalism, which began its development with petty usury capital, is ending its development with gigantic usury capital. 'The French,' says Lysis, 'are the usurers of Europe.' All the conditions of economic life are being profoundly modified by this transformation of capitalism. With a stationary population, and stagnant industry, commerce and shipping, the 'country' can grow rich by usury. 'Fifty persons, representing a capital of eight million francs, can control *2,000 million* francs deposited in four banks.' The 'holding system', with which we are already familiar, leads to the same result. One of the biggest banks, the Société Générale, for instance, issues 64,000 bonds for its 'daughter company', the Egyptian Sugar Refineries. The bonds are issued at 150 per cent, i.e., the bank gains 50 centimes on the franc. The dividends of the new company were found to be fictitious, the 'public' lost from 90 to 100 million francs. 'One of the directors of the Société Générale was a member of the board of directors of the Sugar Refineries.' It is not surprising that the author is driven to the conclusion that 'the French Republic is a financial monarchy'; 'it is the complete domination of the financial oligarchy; the latter dominates over the press and the government.'[9]

The extraordinarily high rate of profit obtained from the issue of bonds, which is one of the principal functions of finance capital, plays a very important part in the development and consolidation of the financial oligarchy. 'There is not a single business of this type within the country that brings in profits even approximately equal to those obtained from the flotation of foreign loans,' says *Die Bank.*[10]

---

[9] Lysis, *Contre l'oligarchie financière en France*, 5 ed. Paris, 1908, pp. 11, 12, 26, 39, 40, 48.

[10] *Die Bank*, 1913, No. 7, S. 630.

'No banking operation brings in profits comparable with those obtained from the issue of securities!' According to the *German Economist*, the average annual profits made on the issue of industrial stock were as follows:

	per cent
1895	38.6
1896	36.1
1897	66.7
1898	67.7
1899	66.9
1900	55.2

'In the ten years from 1891 to 1900, *more than a thousand million marks were 'earned' by issuing German industrial stock.*'[11]

During periods of industrial boom, the profits of finance capital are immense, but during periods of depression, small and unsound businesses go out of existence, and the big banks acquire 'holdings' in them by buying them up for a mere song, or participate in profitable schemes for their 'reconstruction' and 'reorganization'. In the 'reconstruction' of undertakings which have been running at a loss, 'the share capital is written down, that is, profits are distributed on a smaller capital and continue to be calculated on this smaller basis. Or, if the income has fallen to zero, new capital is called in, which, combined with the old and less remunerative capital, will bring in an adequate return.' 'Incidentally,' adds Hilferding, 'all these reorganizations and reconstructions have a twofold significance for the banks: first, as profitable transactions; and secondly, as opportunities for securing control of the companies in difficulties.'[12]

Here is an instance. The Union Mining Company of Dortmund was founded in 1872. Share capital was issued to the amount of nearly 40 million marks and the market price of the shares rose to 170 after it had paid a 12 per cent dividend for its first year. Finance capital skimmed the cream and earned a trifle of something like 28 million marks. The principal

[11] Stillich, op. cit., S. 143, also W. Sombart, *Die deutsche Volkswirtschaft im 19, Jahrhundert,* 2, Aufl., 1909, S. 526, Anlage 8.
[12] *Finance Capital,* p. 172.

sponsor of this company was that very big German Disconto-Gesellschaft which so successfully attained a capital of 300 million marks. Later, the dividends of the Union declined to nil; the shareholders had to consent to a 'writing down' of capital, that is, to losing some of it in order not to lose it all. By a series of 'reconstructions', more than 73 million marks were written off the books of the Union in the course of thirty years. 'At the present time, the original shareholders of the company possess only 5 per cent of the nominal value of their shares'[13] but the banks 'earned something' out of every 'reconstruction'.

Speculation in land situated in the suburbs of rapidly growing big towns is a particularly profitable operation for finance capital. The monopoly of the banks merges here with the monopoly of ground-rent and with monopoly of the means of communication, since the rise in the price of land and the possibility of selling it profitably in lots, etc., is mainly dependent on good means of communication with the centre of the town; and these means of communication are in the hands of large companies which are connected with these same banks through the holding system and the distribution of seats on the boards. As a result we get what the German writer, L. Eschwege, a contributor to *Die Bank* who has made a special study of real estate business and mortgages, etc., calls a 'bog'. Frantic speculation in suburban building lots; collapse of building enterprises like the Berlin firm of Boswau and Knauer, which acquired as much as 100 million marks with the help of the 'sound and solid' Deutsche Bank – the latter, of course, acting through the holding system, i.e., secretly, behind the scenes – and got out of it with a loss of 'only' 12 million marks, then the ruin of small proprietors and of workers who get nothing from the fictitious building firms, fraudulent deals with the 'honest' Berlin police and administration for the purpose of gaining control of the issue of cadastral certificates, building licences, etc.. etc.[14]

'American ethics', which the European professors and well-meaning bourgeois so hypocritically deplore, have, in the age of finance capital, become the ethics of literally every large city in any country.

At the beginning of 1914, there was talk in Berlin of the formation

---

[13] Stillich, op. cit., S. 138 and Liefmann, op. cit., S. 51.
[14] In *Die Bank*, 1913, S. 952, L. Eschwege, *Der Sumpf*; ibid., 1912, 1, S. 223 et seq.

of a 'transport trust', i.e., of establishing 'community of interests' between the three Berlin transport undertakings: the city electric railway, the tramway company and the omnibus company. 'We have been aware,' wrote *Die Bank*, 'that this plan was contemplated ever since it became known that the majority of the shares in the bus company had been acquired by the other two transport companies. . . . We may fully believe those who are pursuing this aim when they say that by uniting the transport services, they will secure economies, part of which will in time benefit the public. But the question is complicated by the fact that behind the transport trust that is being formed are the banks, which, if they desire, can subordinate the means of transportation, which they have monopolized, to the interests of their real estate business. To be convinced of the reasonableness of such a conjecture, we need only recall that the interests of the big bank that encouraged the formation of the Electric Railway Company were already involved in it at the time the company was formed. That is to say: the interests of this transport undertaking were interlocked with the real estate interests. The point is that the eastern line of this railway was to run across land which this bank sold at an enormous profit for itself and for several partners in the transactions when it became certain the line was to be laid down.'[15]

A monopoly, once it is formed and controls thousands of millions, inevitably penetrates into *every* sphere of public life, regardless of the form of government and all other 'details'. In German economic literature one usually comes across obsequious praise of the integrity of the Prussian bureaucracy, and allusions to the French Panama scandal and to political corruption in America. But the fact is that *even* bourgeois literature devoted to German banking matters constantly has to go far beyond the field of purely banking operations; it speaks, for instance, about 'the attraction of the banks' in reference to the increasing frequency with which public officials take employment with the banks, as follows: 'How about the integrity of a state official who in his innermost heart is aspiring to a soft job in the Behrenstrasse?'[16] (The Berlin street where the head office of the Deutsche Bank is situated.) In 1909, the publisher of *Die Bank*, Alfred

---

[15] 'Verkehrstrust' in *Die Bank*, 1914, 1, S. 89.
[16] 'Der Zug zur Bank' in *Die Bank*, 1909, 1, S. 79.

Lansburgh, wrote an article entitled 'The Economic Significance of Byzantinism', in which he incidentally referred to Wilhelm II's tour of Palestine, and to 'the immediate result of this journey, the construction of the Baghdad railway, that fatal 'great product of German enterprise', which is more responsible for the 'encirclement' than all our political blunders put together'.[17] (By encirclement is meant the policy of Edward VII to isolate Germany and surround her with an imperialist anti-German alliance.) In 1911, Eschwege, the contributor to this same magazine to whom I have already referred, wrote an article entitled 'Plutocracy and Bureaucracy', in which he exposed, for example, the case of a German official named Völker, who was a zealous member of the Cartel Committee and who, it turned out some time later, obtained a lucrative post in the biggest cartel, the Steel Syndicate. Similar cases, by no means casual, forced this bourgeois author to admit that 'the economic liberty guaranteed by the German Constitution has become in many departments of economic life, a meaningless phrase' and that under the existing rule of the plutocracy, 'even the widest political liberty cannot save us from being converted into a nation of unfree people'.[18]

As for Russia, I shall confine myself to one example. Some years ago, all the newspapers announced that Davydov, the director of the Credit Department of the Treasury, had resigned his post to take employment with a certain big bank at a salary which, according to the contract, would total over one million rubles in the course of several years. The Credit Department is an institution, the function of which is to 'co-ordinate the activities of all the credit institutions of the country' and which grants subsidies to banks in St. Petersburg and Moscow amounting to between 800 and 1,000 million rubles.[19]

It is characteristic of capitalism in general that the ownership of capital is separated from the application of capital to production, that money capital is separated from industrial or productive capital, and that the rentier who lives entirely on income obtained from money capital, is separated from the entrepreneur and from all who are directly concerned in the management of capital. Imperialism, or the domination of finance

[17] Ibid., S. 301.
[18] Ibid., 1911, 2, S. 825; 1913, 2, S. 962.
[19] E. Agahd, op. cit, S. 202.

capital, is that highest stage of capitalism in which this separation reaches vast proportions. The supremacy of finance capital over all other forms of capital means the predominance of the rentier and of the financial oligarchy; it means that a small number of financially 'powerful' states stand out among all the rest. The extent to which this process is going on may be judged from the statistics on emissions, i.e., the issue of all kinds of securities.

In the *Bulletin of the International Statistical Institute*, A. Neymarck[20] has published very comprehensive, complete and comparative figures covering the issue of securities all over the world, which have been repeatedly quoted in part in economic literature. The following are the totals he gives for four decades:

TOTAL ISSUES IN FRANCS PER DECADE
(*000,000,000*)

1871–80	76.1
1881–90	64.5
1891–1900	100.4
1901–10	197.8

In the 1870s the total amount of issues for the whole world was high, owing particularly to the loans floated in connection with the Franco–Prussian War, and the company-promotion boom which set in in Germany after the war. On the whole, the increase was relatively not very rapid during the three last decades of the nineteenth century, and only in the first ten years of the twentieth century is an enormous increase of almost 100 per cent to be observed. Thus the beginning of the twentieth century marks the turning-point, not only in the growth of monopolies (cartels, syndicates, trusts), of which we have already spoken, but also in the growth of finance capital.

Neymarck estimates the total amount of issued securities current in the world in 1910 at about 815,000 million francs. Deducting from this sum amounts which might have been duplicated, he reduces the total

---

[20] *Bulletin de l'institut international de statistique*, t, XIX, livr. II, La Haye, 1912. Data concerning small states, second column, are estimated by adding 20 per cent to the 1902 figures.

to 575,000–600,000 million, which is distributed among the various countries as follows (I take 600,000 million):

FINANCIAL SECURITIES CURRENT IN 1910
(*000,000,000 francs*)

Great Britain	142		Holland	12.5
United States	132	479	Belgium	7.5
France	110		Spain	7.5
Germany	95		Switzerlan	6.25
Russia	31		Denmark	3.75
Austria-Hungary	24		Sweden, Norway,	
Italy	14		Rumania, etc.	2.5
Japan	12			
			Total	600

From these figures we at once see standing out in sharp relief four of the richest capitalist countries, each of which holds securities to amounts ranging approximately from 100, 000 to 150, 000 million francs. Of these four countries, two, Britain and France, are the oldest capitalist countries, and, as we shall see, possess the most colonies; the other two, the United States and Germany, are capitalist countries leading in the rapidity of development and the degree of extension of capitalist monopolies in industry. Together, these four countries own 479,000 million francs, that is, nearly 80 per cent of the world's finance capital. In one way or another, nearly the whole of the rest of the world is more or less the debtor to and tributary of these international banker countries, these four 'pillars' of world finance capital. It is particularly important to examine the part which the export of capital plays in creating the international network of dependence on and connections of finance capital.

4

EXPORT
OF CAPITAL

Typical of the
old capitalism, when free competition held undivided sway, was the export
of *goods*. Typical of the latest stage of capitalism, when monopolies rule, is
the export of *capital*.

Capitalism is commodity production at its highest stage of
development, when labour-power itself becomes a commodity. The growth
of internal exchange, and, particularly, of international exchange, is a
characteristic feature of capitalism. The uneven and spasmodic development of individual enterprises, individual branches of industry and
individual countries is inevitable under the capitalist system. England
became a capitalist country before any other, and by the middle of the
nineteenth century, having adopted free trade, claimed to be the 'workshop
of the world', the supplier of manufactured goods to all countries, which
in exchange were to keep her provided with raw materials. But in the last
quarter of the nineteenth century, *this* monopoly was already undermined;
for other countries, sheltering themselves with 'protective' tariffs, developed
into independent capitalist states. On the threshold of the twentieth century
we see the formation of a new type of monopoly: firstly, monopolist associations of capitalists in all capitalistically developed countries; secondly,

the monopolist position of a few very rich countries, in which the accumulation of capital has reached gigantic proportions. An enormous 'surplus of capital' has arisen in the advanced countries.

It goes without saying that if capitalism could develop agriculture, which today is everywhere lagging terribly behind industry, if it could raise the living standards of the masses, who in spite of the amazing technical progress are everywhere still half-starved and poverty-stricken, there could be no question of a surplus of capital. This 'argument' is very often advanced by the petty-bourgeois critics of capitalism. But if capitalism did these things it would not be capitalism; for both uneven development and a semi-starvation level of existence of the masses are fundamental and inevitable conditions and constitute premises of this mode of production. As long as capitalism remains what it is, surplus capital will be utilised not for the purpose of raising the standard of living of the masses in a given country, for this would mean a decline in profits for the capitalists, but for the purpose of increasing profits by exporting capital abroad to the backward countries. In these backward countries profits are usually high, for capital is scarce, the price of land is relatively low, wages are low, raw materials are cheap. The export of capital is made possible by a number of backward countries having already been drawn into world capitalist intercourse; main railways have either been or are being built in those countries, elementary conditions for industrial development have been created, etc. The need to export capital arises from the fact that in a few countries capitalism has become 'overripe' and (owing to the backward state of agriculture and the poverty of the masses) capital cannot find a field for 'profitable' investment.

Here are approximate figures showing the amount of capital invested abroad by the three principal countries:[1]

---

[1] Hobson, *Imperialism*, London, 1902, p. 58; Riesser, op. cit., S. 395 und 404; P. Arndt in *Weltwirtschaftliches Archiv*, Bd. 7, 1916, S. 35; Neymarck in *Bulletin;* Hilferding, *Finance Capital*, p. 492; Lloyd George, Speech in the House of Commons, May 4, 1915, reported in the *Daily Telegraph*, May 5, 1915; B. Harms, *Probleme der Weltwirtschaft*, Jena, 1912, S. 235 et seq.; Dr. Siegmund Schilder, *Entwicklungstendenzen der Weltwirtschaft*, Berlin, 1912, Band 1, S. 150; George Paish, 'Great Britain's Capital Investments, etc.', in *Journal of the Royal Statistical Society*, Vol. LXXIV, 1910–11, p. 167 et seq.; Georges Diouritch, *L'Expansion des banques allemandes à l'étranger, ses rapports avec le développement économique de l'Allemagne*, Paris, 1909, p. 84.

CAPITAL INVESTED ABROAD
(*000,000,000 francs*)

Year	Great Britain	France	Germany
1862	3.6	–	–
1872	15.0	10 (1869)	–
1882	22.0	15 (1880)	?
1893	42.0	20 (1890)	?
1902	62.0	27–37	12.5
1914	75–100.0	60	44.0

This table shows that the export of capital reached enormous dimensions only at the beginning of the twentieth century. Before the war the capital invested abroad by the three principal countries amounted to between 175,000 million and 200,000 million francs. At the modest rate of 5 per cent, the income from this sum should reach from 8,000 to 10,000 million francs a year – a sound basis for the imperialist oppression and exploitation of most of the countries and nations of the world, for the capitalist parasitism of a handful of wealthy states!

How is this capital invested abroad distributed among the various countries? *Where* is it invested? Only an approximate answer can be given to these questions, but it is one sufficient to throw light on certain general relations and connections of modern imperialism.

DISTRIBUTION (APPROXIMATE) OF FOREIGN CAPITAL IN
DIFFERENT PARTS OF THE GLOBE
(*circa 1910; 000,000,000 marks*)

	Great Britain	France	Germany	Total
Europe	4	23	18	45
America	37	4	10	51
Asia, Africa and Australia	29	8	7	44
Total	70	35	35	140

The principal spheres of investment of British capital are the British colonies, which are very large also in America (for example, Canada), not to mention Asia, etc. In this case, enormous exports of capital are bound up most closely with vast colonies, of the importance of which for imperialism I shall speak later. In the case of France the situation is different. French capital exports are invested mainly in Europe, primarily in Russia (at least ten thousand million francs). This is mainly *loan* capital, government loans, and not capital invested in industrial undertakings. Unlike British colonial imperialism, French imperialism might be termed usury imperialism. In the case of Germany, we have a third type; colonies are inconsiderable, and German capital invested abroad is divided most evenly between Europe and America.

The export of capital influences and greatly accelerates the development of capitalism in those countries to which it is exported. While, therefore, the export of capital may tend to a certain extent to arrest development in the capital-exporting countries, it can only do so by expanding and deepening the further development of capitalism throughout the world.

The capital-exporting countries are nearly always able to obtain certain 'advantages', the character of which throws light on the peculiarity of the epoch of finance capital and monopoly. The following passage, for instance, appeared in the Berlin review, *Die Bank*, for October 1913:

'A comedy worthy of the pen of Aristophanes is lately being played on the international capital market. Numerous foreign countries, from Spain to the Balkan states, from Russia to Argentina, Brazil and China, are openly or secretly coming into the big money market with demands, sometimes very persistent, for loans. The money markets are not very bright at the moment and the political outlook is not promising. But not a single money market dares to refuse a loan for fear that its neighbour may forestall it, consent to grant a loan and so secure some reciprocal service. In these international transactions the creditor nearly always manages to secure some extra benefit: a favourable clause in a commercial treaty, a coaling station, a contract to construct a harbour, a fat concession, or an order for guns.'[2]

Finance capital has created the epoch of monopolies, and monopolies introduce everywhere monopolist principles: the utilization of 'connections' for profitable transactions takes the place of competition on the open market. The most usual thing is to stipulate that part of the loan granted shall be spent on purchases in the creditor country, particularly on orders for war materials, or for ships, etc. In the course of the last two decades (1890–1910), France has very often resorted to this method. The export of capital thus becomes a means of encouraging the

---

[2] *Die Bank*, 1913, 2, S. 1024–25.

export of commodities. In this connection, transactions between particularly big firms assume a form which, as Schilder[3] 'mildly' puts it, 'borders on corruption'. Krupp in Germany, Schneider in France, Armstrong in Britain are instances of firms which have close connections with powerful banks and governments and which cannot easily be 'ignored' when a loan is being arranged.

France, when granting loans to Russia, 'squeezed' her in the commercial treaty of September 16, 1905, stipulating for certain concessions to run till 1917. She did the same in the commercial treaty with Japan of August 19, 1911. The tariff war between Austria and Serbia, which lasted, with a seven months' interval, from 1906 to 1911, was partly caused by Austria and France competing to supply Serbia with war materials. In January 1912, Paul Deschanel stated in the Chamber of Deputies that from 1908 to 1911 French firms had supplied war materials to Serbia to the value of 45 million francs.

A report from the Austro-Hungarian Consul at San-Paulo (Brazil) states: 'The Brazilian railways are being built chiefly by French, Belgian, British and German capital. In the financial operations connected with the construction of these railways the countries involved stipulate for orders for the necessary railway materials.'

Thus finance capital, literally, one might say, spreads its net over all countries of the world. An important role in this is played by banks founded in the colonies and by their branches. German imperialists look with envy at the 'old' colonial countries which have been particularly 'successful' in providing for themselves in this respect. In 1904, Great Britain had 50 colonial banks with 2,279 branches (in 1910 there were 72 banks with 5,449 branches); France had 20 with 136 branches; Holland, 16 with 68 branches; and Germany had 'only' 13 with 70 branches.[4] The American capitalists, in their turn, are jealous of the English and German: 'In South America,' they complained in 1915, 'five German banks have forty branches and five British banks have seventy branches. . . . Britain and Germany have invested in Argentina, Brazil, and Uruguay in the last twenty-five years approximately four thousand million dollars, and as a

[3] Schilder, op. cit., S. 346, 350, 371.
[4] Riesser, op. cit., 4th ed., S. 375; Diouritch, p. 283.

result together enjoy 46 per cent of the total trade of these three countries.'[5]

The capital-exporting countries have divided the world among themselves in the figurative sense of the term. But finance capital has led to the *actual* division of the world.

[5] *The Annals of the American Academy of Political and Social Science,* Vol. LIX, May 1915, p. 301. In the same volume on p. 331, we read that the well-known statistician Paish, in the last issue of the financial magazine *The Statist,* estimated the amount of capital exported by Britain, Germany, France, Belgium and Holland at $40,000 million, i.e., 200,000 million francs.

5 DIVISION OF THE WORLD AMONG CAPITALIST ASSOCIATIONS

Monopolist capitalist associations, cartels, syndicates and trusts first divided the home market among themselves and obtained more or less complete possession of the industry of their own country. But under capitalism the home market is inevitably bound up with the foreign market. Capitalism long ago created a world market. As the export of capital increased, and as the foreign and colonial connections and 'spheres of influence' of the big monopolist associations expanded in all ways, things 'naturally' gravitated towards an international agreement among these associations, and towards the formation of international cartels.

This is a new stage of world concentration of capital and production, incomparably higher than the preceding stages. Let us see how this supermonopoly develops.

The electrical industry is highly typical of the latest technical achievements and is most typical of capitalism at the *end* of the nineteenth and the beginning of the twentieth centuries. This industry has developed most in the two leaders of the new capitalist countries, the United States and Germany. In Germany, the crisis of 1900 gave a particularly strong impetus to its concentration. During the crisis, the banks, which by that time had become fairly well merged with industry, enormously accelerated and intensified the ruin of relatively small firms and their absorption by the large ones. 'The banks,' writes Jeidels, 'refused a helping hand to the very firms in greatest need of capital, and brought on first a frenzied boom and then the hopeless failure of the companies which had not been connected with them closely enough.'[1]

As a result, after 1900, concentration in Germany progressed with giant strides. Up to 1900 there had been seven or eight 'groups' in the electrical industry. Each consisted of several companies (altogether there were 28) and each was backed by from 2 to 11 banks. Between 1908 and 1912 all these groups were merged into two, or one. The following diagram shows the process.

GROUPS IN THE ELECTRICAL INDUSTRY

Prior to 1900

Felten & Lahmeyer Guillaume	Union A.F.G.	Siemens & Halske	Schuckert & Co.	Bergmann	Kummer
Felten & Lahmeyer	A.E.G. (G.E.C.)	Siemens & Halske-Schuckert		Bergmann	Failed in 1900

By 1912

A.E.G. (G.E.C.) Siemens & Halske-Schuckert

(in close 'co-operation' since 1908)

The famous A.E.G. (General Electric Company), which grew up in this way, controls 175 to 200 companies (through the 'holding' system), and a total capital of approximately 1,500 *million marks.* Of direct agencies abroad alone, it has thirty-four, of which twelve are joint-stock companies, in more than ten countries. As early as 1904 the amount of capital invested abroad by the German electrical industry was estimated at 233 million marks. Of this sum, 62 million were invested in Russia. Needless to say, the A.E.G. is a huge 'combine' – its manufacturing companies alone number no less than sixteen – producing the most diverse articles, from cables and insulators to motor-cars and flying machines.

[1] Jeidels, op. cit., S. 232.

But concentration in Europe was also a component part of the process of concentration in America, which developed in the following way:

General Electric Company		
United States:	Thomson-Houston Co. establishes a firm in Europe	Edison Co. establishes in Europe the French Edison Co. which transfers its patents to the German firm
Germany:	Union Electric Co.	General Electric Co. (A.E.G.)
	General Electric Co. (A.E.G.)	

Thus, *two* electrical 'great powers' were formed: 'there are no other electrical companies in the world *completely* independent of them,' wrote Heinig in his article 'The Path of the Electric Trust'. An idea, although far from complete, of the turnover and the size of the enterprises of the two 'trusts' can be obtained from the following figures:

		Turnover (000,000 marks)	Number of employees	Net profits (000,000 marks)
America: General Electric Co. (G.E.C.)	*1907*	252	28,000	35.4
	1910	298	32,000	45.6
Germany: General Electric Co. (A.E.G.)	*1907*	216	30,700	14.5
	1911	362	60,800	21.7

And then, in 1907, the German and American trusts concluded an agreement by which they divided the world between them. Competition between them ceased. The American General Electric Company (G.E.C.) 'got' the United States and Canada. The German General Electric Company (A.E.G.) 'got' Germany, Austria, Russia, Holland, Denmark, Switzerland, Turkey and the Balkans. Special agreements, naturally secret, were concluded regarding the penetration of 'daughter companies' into new branches of industry, into 'new' countries formally not yet allotted. The two trusts were to exchange inventions and experiments.[2]

---

[2] Riesser, op. cit.; Diouritch, op. cit., p. 239; Kurt Heinig, op. cit.

The difficulty of competing against this trust, actually a single world-wide trust controlling a capital of several thousand million, with 'branches', agencies, representatives, connections, etc., in every corner of the world, is self-evident. But the division of the world between two powerful trusts does not preclude *redivision* if the relation of forces changes as a result of uneven development, war, bankruptcy, etc.

An instructive example of an attempt at such a redivision, of the struggle for redivision, is provided by the oil industry.

'The world oil market,' wrote Jeidels in 1905, 'is even today still divided between two great financial groups – Rockefeller's American Standard Oil Co., and Rothschild and Nobel, the controlling interests of the Russian oilfields in Baku. The two groups are closely connected. But for several years five enemies have been threatening their monopoly':[3] (1) the exhaustion of the American oilfields; (2) the competition of the firm of Mantashev of Baku; (3) the Austrian oilfields; (4) the Rumanian oilfields; (5) the overseas oilfields, particularly in the Dutch colonies (the extremely rich firms, Samuel, and Shell, also connected with British capital). The three last groups are connected with the big German banks, headed by the huge Deutsche Bank. These banks independently and systematically developed the oil industry in Rumania, for example, in order to have a foothold of their 'own'. In 1907, the foreign capital invested in the Rumanian oil industry was estimated at 185 million francs, of which 74 million was German capital.[4]

A struggle began for the 'division of the world', as, in fact, it is called in economic literature. On the one hand, the Rockefeller 'oil trust' wanted to lay its hands on *everything*; it formed a 'daughter company' *right* in Holland, and bought up oilfields in the Dutch Indies, in order to strike at its principal enemy, the Anglo–Dutch Shell trust. On the other hand, the Deutsche Bank and the other German banks aimed at 'retaining' Rumania 'for themselves' and at uniting her with Russia against Rockefeller. The latter possessed far more capital and an excellent system of oil transportation and distribution. The struggle had to end, and did end in 1907, with the utter defeat of the Deutsche Bank, which was confronted with the alternative: either to liquidate its 'oil interests' and lose millions,

---

[3] Jeidels, op. cit., S. 192–93.
[4] Diouritch, op. cit, pp. 245–46.

or submit. It chose to submit, and concluded a very disadvantageous agreement with the 'oil trust'. The Deutsche Bank agreed 'not to attempt anything which might injure American interests'. Provision was made, however, for the annulment of the agreement in the event of Germany establishing a state oil monopoly.

Then the 'comedy of oil' began. One of the German finance kings, von Gwinner, a director of the Deutsche Bank, through his private secretary, Stauss, launched a campaign *for* a state oil monopoly. The gigantic machine of the huge German bank and all its wide 'connections' were set in motion. The press bubbled over with 'patriotic' indignation against the 'yoke' of the American trust, and, on March 15, 1911, the Reichstag, by an almost unanimous vote, adopted a motion asking the government to introduce a bill for the establishment of an oil monopoly. The government seized upon this 'popular' idea, and the game of the Deutsche Bank, which hoped to cheat its American counterpart and improve its business by a state monopoly, appeared to have been won. The German oil magnates already saw visions of enormous profits, which would not be less than those of the Russian sugar refiners. . . . But, firstly, the big German banks quarrelled among themselves over the division of the spoils. The Disconto-Gesellschaft exposed the covetous aims of the Deutsche Bank; secondly, the government took fright at the prospect of a struggle with Rockefeller, for it was very doubtful whether Germany could be sure of obtaining oil from other sources (the Rumanian output was small); thirdly, just at that time the 1913 credits of a thousand million marks were voted for Germany's war preparations. The oil monopoly project was postponed. The Rockefeller 'oil trust' came out of the struggle, for the time being, victorious.

The Berlin review, *Die Bank*, wrote in this connection that Germany could fight the oil trust only by establishing an electricity monopoly and by converting water-power into cheap electricity. 'But,' the author added, 'the electricity monopoly will come when the producers need it, that is to say, when the next great crash in the electrical industry is imminent, and when the gigantic, expensive power stations now being put up at great cost everywhere by private electrical concerns, which are already obtaining certain franchises from towns, from states, etc., can no longer work at a profit. Water-power will then have to be used. But it will be impossible to convert it into cheap electricity as state expense; it will also have to be handed over to a 'private monopoly controlled by the state', because private industry has already concluded a number of contracts and has stipulated for heavy compensation. . . . So it was with the nitrate monopoly, so it is with the oil monopoly, so it will be with the electric power monopoly. It is time our state socialists, who allow themselves to be blinded by a beautiful principle, understood, at last, that in Germany the monopolies have never pursued the aim, nor have they had the result, of benefiting the consumer, or even of handing over to the state part of the promoter's profits; they have served only to facilitate, at the expense of the state, the recovery of private industries which were on the verge of bankruptcy.'[5]

Such are the valuable admissions which the German bourgeois economists are forced to make. We see plainly here how private and state monopolies are interwoven in the epoch of finance capital; how both are but separate links in the imperialist struggle between the big monopolists for the division of the world.

In merchant shipping, the tremendous development of concentration has ended also in the division of the world. In Germany two powerful companies have come to the fore: the Hamburg-Amerika and the Norddeutscher Lloyd, each having a capital of 200 million marks (in stocks and bonds) and possessing shipping tonnage to the value of 185 to 189 million marks. On the other hand, in America, on January 1, 1903, the International Mercantile Marine Co., known as the Morgan trust, was formed; it united nine American and British steamship companies, and possessed a capital of 120 million dollars (480 million marks). As early as 1903, the German giants and this American–British trust concluded an agreement to divide the world with a consequent division of profits. The German companies undertook not to compete in the Anglo–American traffic. Which ports were to be 'allotted' to each was precisely stipulated; a joint committee of control was set up, etc. This agreement was concluded for twenty years, with the prudent provision for its annulment in the event of war.[6]

Extremely instructive also is the story of the formation of the International Rail Cartel. The first attempt of the British, Belgian and German rail manufacturers to form such a cartel was made as early as

---

[5] *Die Bank*, 1912, 1, S. 1036; 1912, 2, S. 629; 1913, 1, S. 388.
[6] Riesser, op. cit., S. 125.

1884, during a severe industrial depression. The manufacturers agreed not to compete with one another in the home markets of the countries involved, and they divided the foreign markets in the following quotas: Great Britain, 66 per cent; Germany, 27 per cent; Belgium, 7 per cent. India was reserved entirely for Great Britain. Joint war was declared against a British firm which remained outside the cartel, the cost of which was met by a percentage levy on all sales. But in 1886 the cartel collapsed when two British firms retired from it. It is characteristic that agreement could not be achieved during subsequent boom periods.

At the beginning of 1904, the German steel syndicate was formed. In November 1904, the International Rail Cartel was revived, with the following quotas: Britain, 53.5 per cent; Germany, 28.83 per cent; Belgium, 17.67 per cent. France came in later and received 4.8 per cent, 5.8 per cent and 6.4 per cent in the first, second and third year respectively, over and above the 100 per cent limit, i.e., out of a total of 104.8 per cent, etc. In 1905, the United States Steel Corporation entered the cartel; then Austria and Spain. 'At the present time,' wrote Vogelstein in 1910, 'the division of the world is complete, and the big consumers, primarily the state railways – since the world has been parcelled out without consideration for their interests – can now dwell like the poet in the heavens of Jupiter.'[7]

Let me also mention the International Zinc Syndicate which was established in 1909 and which precisely apportioned output among five groups of factories: German, Belgian, French, Spanish and British; and also the International Dynamite Trust, which, Liefmann says, is 'quite a modern, close alliance of all the German explosives manufacturers who, with the French and American dynamite manufacturers, organized in a similar manner, have divided the whole world among themselves, so to speak'.[8]

Liefmann calculated that in 1897 there were altogether about forty international cartels in which Germany had a share, while in 1910 there were about a hundred.

Certain bourgeois writers (now joined by Karl Kautsky, who has completely abandoned the Marxist position he had held, for example, in 1909) have expressed the opinion that international cartels, being one of

[7] Vogelstein, *Organisationsformen*, S. 100.
[8] Liefmann, *Kartelle und Trusts*, 2. A.. S. 161.

the most striking expressions of the internationalization of capital, give the hope of peace among nations under capitalism. Theoretically, this opinion is absolutely absurd, while in practice it is sophistry and a dishonest defence of the worst opportunism. International cartels show to what point capitalist monopolies have developed, and *the object* of the struggle between the various capitalist associations. This last circumstance is the most important; it alone shows us the historico-economic meaning of what is taking place; for the *forms* of the struggle may and do constantly change in accordance with varying, relatively specific and temporary causes, but the *substance* of the struggle, its class *content*, positively *cannot* change while classes exist. Naturally, it is in the interests of, for example, the German bourgeoisie, to whose side Kautsky has in effect gone over in his theoretical arguments (I shall deal with this later), to obscure the *substance* of the present economic struggle (the division of the world) and to emphasize now this and now another *form* of the struggle. Kautsky makes the same mistake. Of course, we have in mind not only the German bourgeoisie, but the bourgeoisie all over the world. The capitalists divide the world, not out of any particular malice, but because the degree of concentration which has been reached forces them to adopt this method in order to obtain profits. And they divide it 'in proportion to capital', 'in proportion to strength', because there cannot be any other method of division under commodity production and capitalism. But strength varies with the degree of economic and political development. In order to understand what is taking place, it is necessary to know what questions are settled by the changes in strength. The question as to whether these changes are 'purely' economic or *non*-economic (e.g., military) is a secondary one, which cannot in the least affect fundamental views on the latest epoch of capitalism. To substitute the question of the form of the struggle and agreements (today peaceful, tomorrow warlike, the next day warlike again) for the question of the *substance* of the struggle and agreements between capitalist associations is to sink to the role of a sophist.

The epoch of the latest stage of capitalism shows us that certain relations between capitalist associations grow up, *based* on the economic division of the world; while parallel to and in connection with it, certain relations grow up between political alliances, between states, on the basis of the territorial division of the world, of the struggle for colonies, of the 'struggle for spheres of influence'.

6

DIVISION OF THE WORLD AMONG THE GREAT POWERS

In his book,
on 'the territorial development of the European colonies', A. Supan,[1] the geographer, gives the following brief summary of this development at the end of the nineteenth century:

PERCENTAGE OF TERRITORY BELONGING TO
THE EUROPEAN COLONIAL POWERS
(*Including the United States*)

	1876	1900	Increase or decrease
Africa	10.8	90.4	+79.6
Polynesia	56.8	98.9	+42.1
Asia	51.5	56.6	+5.1
Australia	100.0	100.0	–
America	27.5	27.2	– 0.3

'The characteristic feature of this period,' he concludes, therefore, 'is the division of Africa and Polynesia.' As there are no unoccupied territories – that is, territories that do not belong to any state – in Asia and

---

[1] A. Supan, *Die territoriale Entwickhmg der europäischen Kolonien*, 1906, S. 254.

America, it is necessary to amplify Supan's conclusion and say that the characteristic feature of the period under review is the final partitioning of the globe –final, not in the sense that *repartition* is impossible; on the contrary, repartitions are possible and inevitable – but in the sense that the colonial policy of the capitalist countries has *completed* the seizure of the unoccupied territories on our planet. For the first time the world is completely divided up, so that in the future *only* redivision is possible, i.e., territories can only pass from one 'owner' to another, instead of passing as ownerless territory to an 'owner'.

Hence, we are living in a peculiar epoch of world colonial policy, which is most closely connected with the 'latest stage in the development of capitalism', with finance capital. For this reason, it is essential first of all to deal in greater detail with the facts, in order to ascertain as exactly as possible what distinguishes this epoch from those preceding it, and what the present situation is. In the first place, two questions of fact arise here: is an intensification of colonial policy, a sharpening of the struggle for colonies, observed precisely in the epoch of finance capital? And how, in this respect, is the world divided at the present time?

The American writer, Morris, in his book on the history of colonization,[2] made an attempt to sum up the data on the colonial possessions of Great Britain, France and Germany during different periods of the nineteenth century. The following is a brief summary of the results he has obtained:

COLONIAL POSSESSIONS

Year	Great Britain		France		Germany	
	Area (*000,000 sq. m.*)	Pop. (*000,000*)	Area (*000,000 sq. m.*)	Pop. (*000,000*)	Area (*000,000 sq. m.*)	Pop. (*000,000*)
1815–30	?	126.4	0.02	0.5	–	–
1860	2.5	145.1	0.2	3.4	–	–
1880	7.7	267.9	0.7	7.5	–	–
1899	9.3	309.0	3.7	56.4	1.0	14.7

[2] Henry C. Morris, *The History of Colonization*, New York, 1900, Vol. II. p. 88; Vol. I, p. 419; Vol. II, p. 304.

For Great Britain, the period of the enormous expansion of colonial conquests was that between 1860 and 1880, and it was also very considerable in the last twenty years of the nineteenth century. For France and Germany this period falls precisely in these twenty years. We saw above that the development of pre-monopoly capitalism, of capitalism in which free competition was predominant, reached its limit in the 1860s and 1870s. We now see that it is *precisely after that period* that the tremendous 'boom' in colonial conquests begins, and that the struggle for the territorial division of the world becomes extraordinarily sharp. It is beyond doubt, therefore, that capitalism's transition to the stage of monopoly capitalism, to finance capital, *is connected* with the intensification of the struggle for the partitioning of the world.

Hobson, in his work on imperialism, marks the years 1884–1900 as the epoch of intensified 'expansion' of the chief European states. According to his estimate, Great Britain during these years acquired 3,700,000 square miles of territory with 57,000,000 inhabitants; France, 3,600,000 square miles with 36,500,000: Germany, 1,000,000 square miles with 14,700,000; Belgium, 900,000 square miles with 30,000,000; Portugal, 800,000 square miles with 9,000,000 inhabitants. The scramble for colonies by all the capitalist states at the end of the nineteenth century and particularly since the 1880s is a commonly known fact in the history of diplomacy and of foreign policy.

In the most flourishing period of free competition in Great Britain, i.e., between 1840 and 1860, the leading British bourgeois politicians were *opposed* to colonial policy and were of the opinion that the liberation of the colonies, their complete separation from Britain, was inevitable and desirable. M. Beer, in an article, 'Modern British Imperialism',[3] published in 1898, shows that in 1852, Disraeli, a statesman who was generally inclined towards imperialism,. declared: 'The colonies are millstones round our necks.' But at the end of the nineteenth century the British heroes of the hour were Cecil Rhodes and Joseph Chamberlain, who openly advocated imperialism and applied the imperialist policy in the most cynical manner!

It is not without interest to observe that even then these leading British bourgeois politicians saw the connection between what might be

---

[3] *Die Neue Zeit*, XVI, I, 1898, S. 302.

called the purely economic and the socio-political roots of modern imperialism. Chamberlain advocated imperialism as a 'true, wise and economical policy', and pointed particularly to the German, American and Belgian competition which Great Britain was encountering in the world market. Salvation lies in monopoly, said the capitalists as they formed cartels, syndicates and trusts. Salvation lies in monopoly, echoed the political leaders of the bourgeoisie, hastening to appropriate the parts of the world not yet shared out. And Cecil Rhodes, we are informed by his intimate friend, the journalist Stead, expressed his imperialist views to him in 1895 in the following terms: 'I was in the East End of London [a working-class quarter] yesterday and attended a meeting of the unemployed. I listened to the wild speeches, which were just a cry for 'bread! bread!' and on my way home I pondered over the scene and I became more than ever convinced of the importance of imperialism. . . . My cherished idea is a solution for the social problem, i.e., in order to save the 40,000,000 inhabitants of the United Kingdom from a bloody civil war, we colonial statesmen must acquire new lands to settle the surplus population, to provide new markets for the goods produced in the factories and mines. The Empire, as I have always said, is a bread and butter question. If you want to avoid civil war, you must become imperialists.'[4]

That was said in 1895 by Cecil Rhodes, millionaire, a king of finance, the man who was mainly responsible for the Anglo–Boer War. True, his defence of imperialism is crude and cynical, but in substance it does not differ from the 'theory' advocated by Messrs. Maslov, Südekum, Potresov, David, the founder of Russian Marxism and others. Cecil Rhodes was a somewhat more honest social-chauvinist. . . .

To present as precise a picture as possible of the territorial division of the world and of the changes which have occurred during the last decades in this respect, I shall utilize the data furnished by Supan in the work already quoted on the colonial possessions of all the powers of the world. Supan takes the years 1876 and 1900; I shall take the year 1876 – a year very aptly selected, for it is precisely by that time that the pre-monopolist stage of development of West-European capitalism can be said to have been, in the main, completed – and the year 1914, and instead of Supan's figures I shall quote the more recent statistics of Hübner's *Geographical and*

---

[4] Ibid., S, 304.

Statistical Tables, Supan gives figures only for colonies; I think it useful, in order to present a complete picture of the division of the world, to add brief data on non-colonial and semi-colonial countries, in which category I place Persia, China and Turkey: the first of these countries is already almost completely a colony, the second and third are becoming such.

We thus get the following result:

COLONIAL POSSESSIONS OF THE GREAT POWERS
(*000,000 square kilometres and 000,000 inhabitants*)

	Colonies				Metropolitan countries		Total	
	1876		1914		1914		1914	
	Area	Pop.	Area	Pop.	Area	Pop.	Area	Pop.
Great Britain	22.5	251.9	33.5	393.5	0.3	46.5	33.8	440.0
Russia	17.0	15.9	17.4	33.2	5.4	136.2	22.8	169.4
France	0.9	6.0	10.6	55.5	0.5	39.6	11.1	95.1
Germany	–	–	2.9	12.3	0.5	64.9	3.4	77.2
United States	–	–	0.3	9.7	9.4	97.0	9.7	106.7
Japan	–	–	0.3	19.2	0.4	53.0	0.7	72.2
Total for six Great Powers	40.4	273.8	65.0	523.4	16.5	437.2	81.5	960.6
Colonies of other powers (Belgium, Holland, etc.)					9.9		45.3	
Semi-colonial countries (Persia, China, Turkey)					14.5		361.2	
Other countries					28.0		289.9	
Total for the world					133.9		1,657.0	

We clearly see from these figures how 'complete' was the partition of the world at the turn of the twentieth century. After 1876 colonial possessions increased to enormous dimensions, by more than fifty per cent, from 40,000,000 to 65,000,000 square kilometres for the six biggest powers; the increase amounts to 25, 000, 000 square kilometres, fifty per cent more than the area of the metropolitan countries (16, 500, 000 square kilometres). In 1876 three powers had no colonies, and a fourth, France, had scarcely any. By 1914 these four powers had acquired colonies with an area of 14,100,000 square kilometres, i.e., about half as much again as the area of Europe, with a population of nearly 100,000,000. The unevenness in the rate of expansion of colonial possessions is very great. If, for instance, we compare France, Germany and Japan, which do not differ very much in area and population, we see that the first has acquired almost three times as much colonial territory as the other two combined. In regard to finance capital, France, at the beginning of the period we are considering, was also, perhaps, several times richer than Germany and Japan put together. In addition to, and on the basis of, purely economic conditions, geographical and other conditions also affect the dimensions of colonial possessions. However strong the process of levelling the world, of levelling the economic and living conditions in different countries, may have been in the past decades as a result of the pressure of large-scale industry, exchange and finance capital, considerable differences still remain; and among the six countries mentioned we see, firstly, young capitalist countries (America, Germany, Japan) whose progress has been extraordinarily rapid; secondly, countries with an old capitalist development (France and Great Britain), whose progress lately has been much slower than that of the previously mentioned countries, and thirdly, a country most backward economically (Russia), where modern capitalist imperialism is enmeshed, so to speak, in a particularly close network of pre-capitalist relations.

Alongside the colonial possessions of the Great Powers, we have placed the small colonies of the small states, which are, so to speak, the next objects of a possible and probable 'redivision' of colonies. These small states mostly retain their colonies only because the big powers are torn by conflicting interests, friction, etc., which prevent them from coming to an agreement on the division of the spoils. As to the 'semi-colonial' states, they provide an example of the transitional forms which are to be found in all spheres of nature and society. Finance capital is such a great, such a decisive, you might say, force in all economic and in all international relations, that it is capable of subjecting, and actually does subject, to itself even states enjoying the fullest political independence; we shall shortly see examples of this. Of course, finance capital finds most 'convenient', and derives the greatest profit from, a *form* of subjection which involves the loss of the political independence of the subjected countries and peoples. In this respect, the semi-colonial countries provide a typical example of the 'middle stage'. It is natural that the struggle for these semi-dependent countries should have become particularly bitter in the epoch of finance capital, when the rest of the world has already been divided up.

Colonial policy and imperialism existed before the latest stage of capitalism, and even before capitalism. Rome, founded on slavery, pursued a colonial policy and practised imperialism. But 'general' disquisitions on imperialism, which ignore, or put into the background, the fundamental difference between socio-economic formations, inevitably turn into the most vapid banality or bragging, like the comparison: 'Greater Rome and Greater Britain.'[5] Even the capitalist colonial policy of *previous* stages of capitalism is essentially different from the colonial policy of finance capital.

The principal feature of the latest stage of capitalism is the domination of monopolist associations of big employers. These monopolies are most firmly established when *all* the sources of raw materials are captured by one group, and we have seen with what zeal the international capitalist associations exert every effort to deprive their rivals of all opportunity of competing, to buy up, for example, ironfields, oilfields, etc. Colonial possession alone gives the monopolies complete guarantee against all contingencies in the struggle against competitors, including the case of the adversary wanting to be protected by a law establishing a state monopoly. The more capitalism is developed, the more strongly the shortage of raw materials is felt, the more intense the competition and the hunt for sources of raw materials throughout the whole world, the more desperate the struggle for the acquisition of colonies.

'It may be asserted,' writes Schilder, 'although it may sound paradoxical to some, that in the more or less foreseeable future the growth of the urban and industrial population is more likely to be hindered by a shortage of raw materials for industry than by a shortage of food.' For example, there is a growing shortage of timber – the price of which is steadily rising – of leather, and of raw materials for the textile industry. 'Associations of manufacturers are making efforts to create an equilibrium between agriculture and industry in the whole of world economy; as an example of this we might mention the International Federation of Cotton Spinners' Associations in several of the most important industrial countries, founded in 1904, and the European Federation of Flax Spinners' Associations, founded on the same model in 1910.'[6]

Of course, the bourgeois reformists, and among them particularly the present-day adherents of Kautsky, try to belittle the importance of

---

[5] C.P. Lucas, *Greater Rome and Greater Britain*, Oxford, 1912, or the Earl of Cromer's *Ancient and Modern Imperialism*, London, 1910.

[6] Schilder, op. cit., S. 38–42.

facts of this kind by arguing that raw materials 'could be' obtained in the open market without a 'costly and dangerous' colonial policy; and that the supply of raw materials 'could be' increased enormously by 'simply' improving conditions in agriculture in general. But such arguments become an apology for imperialism, an attempt to paint it in bright colours, because they ignore the principal feature of the latest stage of capitalism: monopolies. The free market is becoming more and more a thing of the past; monopolist syndicates and trusts are restricting it with every passing day, and 'simply' improving conditions in agriculture means improving the conditions of the masses, raising wages and reducing profits. Where, except in the imagination of sentimental reformists, are there any trusts capable of concerning themselves with the condition of the masses instead of the conquest of colonies?

Finance capital is interested not only in the already discovered sources of raw materials but also in potential sources, because present-day technical development is extremely rapid, and land which is useless today may be improved tomorrow if new methods are devised (to this end a big bank can equip a special expedition of engineers, agricultural experts, etc.), and if large amounts of capital are invested. This also applies to prospecting for minerals, to new methods of processing up and utilizing raw materials, etc., etc. Hence, the inevitable striving of finance capital to enlarge its spheres of influence and even its actual territory. In the same way that the trusts capitalize their property at two or three times its value, taking into account its 'potential' (and not actual) profits and the further results of monopoly, so finance capital in general strives to seize the largest possible amount of land of all kinds in all places, and by every means, taking into account potential sources of raw materials and fearing to be left behind in the fierce struggle for the last remnants of independent territory, or for the repartition of those territories that have been already divided.

The British capitalists are exerting every effort to develop cotton growing in *their* colony, Egypt (in 1904, out of 2,300,000 hectares of land under cultivation, 600,000, or more than one-fourth, were under cotton); the Russians are doing the same in *their* colony, Turkestan, because in this way they will be in a better position to defeat their foreign competitors, to monopolize the sources of raw materials and form a more economical and profitable textile trust in which *all* the processes of cotton production and manufacturing will be 'combined' and concentrated in the hands of one set of owners.

The interests pursued in exporting capital also give an impetus to the conquest of colonies, for in the colonial market it is easier to employ monopoly methods (and sometimes they are the only methods that can be employed) to eliminate competition, to ensure supplies, to secure the necessary 'connections', etc.

The non-economic superstructure which grows up on the basis of finance capital, its politics and its ideology, stimulates the striving for colonial conquest. 'Finance capital does not want liberty, it wants domination,' as Hilferding very truly says. And a French bourgeois writer, developing and supplementing, as it were, the ideas of Cecil Rhodes quoted above,[7] writes that social causes should be added to the economic causes of modern colonial policy: 'Owing to the growing complexities of life and the difficulties which weigh not only on the masses of the workers, but also on the middle classes, "impatience, irritation and hatred are accumulating in all the countries of the old civilization and are becoming a menace to public order; the energy which is being hurled out of the definite class channel must be given employment abroad in order to avert an explosion at home".'[8]

Since we are speaking of colonial policy in the epoch of capitalist imperialism, it must be observed that finance capital and its foreign policy, which is the struggle of the great powers for the economic and political division of the world, give rise to a number of *transitional* forms of state dependence. Not only are the two main groups of countries, those owning colonies, and the colonies themselves, but also the diverse forms of dependent countries which, politically, are formally independent, but in fact, are enmeshed in the net of financial and diplomatic dependence, typical of this epoch. We have already referred to one form of dependence – the semi-colony. An example of another is provided by Argentina.

'South America, and especially Argentina,' writes Schulze-Gaevernitz in his work on British imperialism, 'is so dependent financially on London that it ought to be described as almost a British commercial

[7] *Die Neue Zeit*, XVI, I, 1898, S 302.
[8] Wahl, *La France aux colonies* quoted by Henri Russier, *Le Portage de l'Oceame*, Paris, 1905, p. 165.

colony.'[9] Basing himself on the reports of the Austro-Hungarian Consul at Buenos Aires for 1909, Schilder estimated the amount of British capital invested in Argentina at 8,750 million francs. It is not difficult to imagine what strong connections British finance capital (and its faithful 'friend', diplomacy) thereby acquires with the Argentine bourgeoisie, with the circles that control the whole of that country's economic and political life.

A somewhat different form of financial and diplomatic dependence, accompanied by political independence, is presented by Portugal. Portugal is an independent sovereign state, but actually, for more than two hundred years, since the war of the Spanish Succession (1701–14), it has been a British protectorate. Great Britain has protected Portugal and her colonies in order to fortify her own positions in the fight against her rivals, Spain and France. In return Great Britain has received commercial privileges, preferential conditions for importing goods and especially capital into Portugal and the Portuguese colonies, the right to use the ports and islands of Portugal, her telegraph cables, etc., etc.[10] Relations of this kind have always existed between big and little states, but in the epoch of capitalist imperialism they become a general system, they form part of the sum total of 'divide the world' relations and become links in the chain of operations of world finance capital.

In order to finish with the question of the division of the world, I must make the following additional observation. This question was raised quite openly and definitely not only in American literature after the Spanish–American War, and in English literature after the Anglo–Boer War, at the very end of the nineteenth century and the beginning of the twentieth; not only has German literature, which has 'most jealously' watched 'British imperialism', systematically given its appraisal of this fact. This question has also been raised in French bourgeois literature as definitely and broadly as is thinkable from the bourgeois point of view. Let me quote Driault, the historian, who, in his book, *Political and Social Problems at the End of the Nineteenth Century*, in the chapter 'The Great Powers and the Division of the World', wrote the following: 'During the past few years, all the free territory of the globe, with the exception of

[9] Schultze-Gaevernitz, *Britischer Imperialismus und englischer Freihandel zu Beginn des 20-ten Jahrhunderts*, Leipzig, 1906, S. 318. Sartorius v. Waltershausen says the same in *Das volkswirtschaftliche System der Kapitalanlage im Auslande*, Berlin, 1907, S. 46.

[10] Schilder, op. cit. Vol. I, S. 160–61.

China, has been occupied by the powers of Europe and North America. This has already brought about several conflicts and shifts of spheres of influence, and these foreshadow more terrible upheavals in the near future. For it is necessary to make haste. The nations which have not yet made provision for themselves run the risk of never receiving their share and never participating in the tremendous exploitation of the globe which will be one of the most essential features of the next century [i.e., the twentieth]. That is why all Europe and America have lately been afflicted with the fever of colonial expansion, of 'imperialism', that most noteworthy feature of the end of the nineteenth century.' And the author added: 'In this partition of the world, in this furious hunt for the treasures and the big markets of the globe, the relative strength of the empires founded in this nineteenth century is totally out of proportion to the place occupied in Europe by the nations which founded them. The dominant powers in Europe, the arbiters of her destiny, are *not* equally preponderant in the whole world. And, as colonial might, the hope of controlling as yet unassessed wealth, will evidently react upon the relative strength of the European powers, the colonial question – 'imperialism', if you will – which has already modified the political conditions of Europe itself, will modify them more and more.'[11]

[11] J.-E. Driault, *Problèmes politiques et sociaux*, Paris, 1900, p. 299.

7 IMPERIALISM, AS A SPECIAL STAGE OF CAPITALISM

We must now
try to sum up, to draw together the threads of what has been said above on the subject of imperialism. Imperialism emerged as the development and direct continuation of the fundamental characteristics of capitalism in general. But capitalism only became capitalist imperialism at a definite and very high stage of its development, when certain of its fundamental characteristics began to change into their opposites, when the features of the epoch of transition from capitalism to a higher social and economic system had taken shape and revealed themselves in all spheres. Economically, the main thing in this process is the displacement of capitalist free competition by capitalist monopoly. Free competition is the basic feature of capitalism, and of commodity production generally; monopoly is the exact opposite of free competition, but we have seen the latter being transformed into monopoly before our eyes, creating large-scale industry and forcing out small industry, replacing large-scale by still larger-scale industry, and carrying concentration of production and capital to the point where out of it has grown and is growing monopoly: cartels, syndicates and trusts, and merging with them, the capital of a dozen or so banks, which manipulate thousands of millions. At the same time the monopolies,

which have grown out of free competition, do not eliminate the latter, but exist above it and alongside it, and thereby give rise to a number of very acute, intense antagonisms, frictions and conflicts. Monopoly is the transition from capitalism to a higher system.

If it were necessary to give the briefest possible definition of imperialism we should have to say that imperialism is the monopoly stage of capitalism. Such a definition would include what is most important, for, on the one hand, finance capital is the bank capital of a few very big monopolist banks, merged with the capital of the monopolist associations of industrialists; and, on the other hand, the division of the world is the transition from a colonial policy which has extended without hindrance to territories unseized by any capitalist power, to a colonial policy of monopolist possession of the territory of the world, which has been completely divided up.

But very brief definitions, although convenient, for they sum up the main points, are nevertheless inadequate, since we have to deduce from them some especially important features of the phenomenon that has to be defined. And so, without forgetting the conditional and relative value of all definitions in general, which can never embrace all the concatenations of a phenomenon in its full development, we must give a definition of imperialism that will include the following five of its basic features:

(1) The concentration of production and capital has developed to such a high stage that it has created monopolies which play a decisive role in economic life; (2) the merging of bank capital with industrial capital, and the creation, on the basis of this 'finance capital', of a financial oligarchy; (3) the export of capital as distinguished from the export of commodities acquires exceptional importance; (4) the formation of international monopolist capitalist associations which share the world among themselves, and (5) the territorial division of the whole world among the biggest capitalist powers is completed. Imperialism is capitalism at that stage of development at which the dominance of monopolies and finance capital is established; in which the export of capital has acquired pronounced importance; in which the division of the world among the international trusts has begun, in which the division of all territories of the globe among the biggest capitalist powers has been completed.

We shall see later that imperialism can and must be defined differently if we bear in mind not only the basic, purely economic concepts

– to which the above definition is limited – but also the historical place of this stage of capitalism in relation to capitalism in general, or the relation between imperialism and the two main trends in the working-class movement. The thing to be noted at this point is that imperialism, as interpreted above, undoubtedly represents a special stage in the development of capitalism. To enable the reader to obtain the most well-grounded idea of imperialism, I deliberately tried to quote as extensively as possible *bourgeois* economists who have to admit the particularly incontrovertible facts concerning the latest stage of capitalist economy. With the same object in view, I have quoted detailed statistics which enable one to see to what degree bank capital, etc., has grown, in what precisely the transformation of quantity into quality, of developed capitalism into imperialism, was expressed. Needless to say, of course, all boundaries in nature and in society are conventional and changeable, and it would be absurd to argue, for example, about the particular year or decade in which imperialism 'definitely' became established.

In the matter of defining imperialism, however, we have to enter into controversy, primarily, with Karl Kautsky, the principal Marxist theoretician of the epoch of the so-called Second International – that is, of the twenty-five years between 1889 and 1914. The fundamental ideas expressed in our definition of imperialism were very resolutely attacked by Kautsky in 1915, and even in November 1914, when he said that imperialism must not be regarded as a 'phase' or stage of economy, but as a policy, a definite policy 'preferred' by finance capital; that imperialism must not be 'identified' with 'present-day capitalism'; that if imperialism is to be understood to mean 'all the phenomena of present-day capitalism' – cartels, protection, the domination of the financiers, and colonial policy – then the question as to whether imperialism is necessary to capitalism becomes reduced to the 'flattest tautology', because, in that case, 'imperialism is naturally a vital necessity for capitalism', and so on. The best way to present Kautsky's idea is to quote his own definition of imperialism, which is diametrically opposed to the substance of the ideas which I have set forth (for the objections coming from the camp of the German Marxists, who have been advocating similar ideas for many years already, have been long known to Kautsky as the objections of a definite trend in Marxism).

Kautsky's definition is as follows:

'Imperialism is a product of highly developed industrial capitalism. It consists in the striving of every industrial capitalist nation to bring under its control or to annex all large areas of *agrarian* [Kautsky's italics] territory, irrespective of what nations inhabit it.'[1]

This definition is of no use at all because it one-sidedly, i.e., arbitrarily, singles out only the national question (although the latter is extremely important in itself as well as in its relation to imperialism), it arbitrarily and *inaccurately* connects this question *only* with industrial capital in the countries which annex other nations, and in an equally arbitrary and inaccurate manner pushes into the forefront the annexation of agrarian regions.

Imperialism is a striving for annexations – this is what the *political* part of Kautsky's definition amounts to. It is correct, but very incomplete, for politically, imperialism is, in general, a striving towards violence and reaction. For the moment, however, we are interested in the *economic* aspect of the question, which Kautsky *himself* introduced into *his* definition. The inaccuracies in Kautsky's definition are glaring. The characteristic feature of imperialism is *not* industrial *but* finance capital. It is not an accident that in France it was precisely the extraordinarily rapid development of *finance* capital, and the weakening of industrial capital, that from the eighties onwards gave rise to the extreme intensification of annexationist (colonial) policy. The characteristic feature of imperialism is precisely that it strives to annex *not only* agrarian territories, but even most highly industrialized regions (German appetite for Belgium; French appetite for Lorraine), because (1) the fact that the world is already partitioned obliges those contemplating a *redivision* to reach out for *every kind* of territory, and (2) an essential feature of imperialism is the rivalry between several great powers in the striving for hegemony, i.e., for the conquest of territory, not so much directly for themselves as to weaken the adversary and undermine *his* hegemony. (Belgium is particularly important for Germany as a base for operations against Britain; Britain needs Baghdad as a base for operations against Germany, etc.)

Kautsky refers especially – and repeatedly – to English writers who, he alleges, have given a purely political meaning to the word 'imperialism' in the sense that he, Kautsky, understands it. We take up the work by

---

[1] *Die Neue Zeit*, 1914, 2 (B. 32), S. 909. Sept. 11, 1914; cf. 1915. 2, S. 107 et seq.

the English writer Hobson, *Imperialism*, which appeared in 1902, and there we read:

'The new imperialism differs from the older, first, in substituting for the ambition of a single growing empire the theory and the practice of competing empires, each motivated by similar lusts of political aggrandizement and commercial gain; secondly, in the dominance of financial or investing over mercantile interests.'[2]

We see that Kautsky is absolutely wrong in referring to English writers generally (unless he meant the vulgar English imperialists, or the avowed apologists for imperialism). We see that Kautsky, while claiming that he continues to advocate Marxism, as a matter of fact takes a step backward compared with the *social-liberal* Hobson, who *more correctly* takes into account two 'historically concrete' (Kautsky's definition is a mockery of historical concreteness!) features of modern imperialism: (1) the competition between *several* imperialisms, and (2) the predominance of the financier over the merchant. If it is chiefly a question of the annexation of agrarian countries by industrial countries, then the role of the merchant is put in the forefront.

Kautsky's definition is not only wrong and un-Marxist. It serves as a basis for a whole system of views which signify a rupture with Marxist theory and Marxist practice all along the line. I shall refer to this later. The argument about words which Kautsky raises as to whether the latest stage of capitalism should be called imperialism or the stage of finance capital is not worth serious attention. Call it what you will, it makes no difference. The essence of the matter is that Kautsky detaches the politics of imperialism from its economics, speaks of annexations as being a policy 'preferred' by finance capital, and opposes to it another bourgeois policy which, he alleges, is possible on this very same basis of finance capital. It follows, then, that monopolies in the economy are compatible with non-monopolistic, non-violent, non-annexationist methods in politics. It follows, then, that the territorial division of the world, which was completed during this very epoch of finance capital, and which constitutes the basis of the present peculiar forms of rivalry between the biggest capitalist states, is compatible with a non-imperialist policy. The result is a slurring-over and a blunting of the most profound contradictions of the latest stage of

[2] Hobson, *Imperialism*, London, 1902, p. 324.

capitalism, instead of an exposure of their depth; the result is bourgeois reformism instead of Marxism.

Kautsky enters into controversy with the German apologist of imperialism and annexations, Cunow, who clumsily and cynically argues that imperialism is present-day capitalism; the development of capitalism is inevitable and progressive; therefore imperialism is progressive; therefore, we should grovel before it and glorify it! This is something like the caricature of the Russian Marxists which the Narodniks drew in 1894–95. They argued: if the Marxists believe that capitalism is inevitable in Russia, that it is progressive, then they ought to open a tavern and begin to implant capitalism! Kautsky's reply to Cunow is as follows: imperialism is not present-day capitalism; it is only one of the forms of the policy of present-day capitalism. This policy we can and should fight, fight imperialism, annexations, etc.

The reply seems quite plausible, but in effect it is a more subtle and more disguised (and therefore more dangerous) advocacy of conciliation with imperialism, because a 'fight' against the policy of the trusts and banks that does not affect the economic basis of the trusts and banks is mere bourgeois reformism and pacifism, the benevolent and innocent expression of pious wishes. Evasion of existing contradictions, forgetting the most important of them, instead of revealing their full depth – such is Kautsky's theory, which has nothing in common with Marxism. Naturally, such a 'theory' can only serve the purpose of advocating unity with the Cunows!

'From the purely economic point of view,' writes Kautsky, 'it is not impossible that capitalism will yet go through a new phase, that of the extension of the policy of the cartels to foreign policy, the phase of ultra-imperialism,'[3] i.e., of a superimperialism, of a union of the imperialisms of the whole world and not struggles among them, a phase when wars shall cease under capitalism, a phase of 'the joint exploitation of the world by internationally united finance capital'.[4]

We shall have to deal with this 'theory of ultra-imperialism' later on in order to show in detail how decisively and completely it breaks with Marxism. At present, in keeping with the general plan of the present work,

---

[3] *Die Neue Zeit*, 1914, 2 (B. 32), S. 921. Sept, 11, 1914. Cf. 1915, 2, S. 107 et seq.
[4] Ibid., 1915, 1. S. 144, April 30, 1915.

we must examine the exact economic data on this question. 'From the purely economic point of view', is 'ultra-imperialism' possible, or is it ultra-nonsense?

If the purely economic point of view is meant to be a 'pure' abstraction, then all that can be said reduces itself to the following proposition: development is proceeding towards monopolies, hence, towards a single world monopoly, towards a single world trust. This is indisputable, but it is also as completely meaningless as is the statement that 'development is proceeding' towards the manufacture of foodstuffs in laboratories. In this sense the 'theory' of ultra-imperialism is no less absurd than a 'theory of ultra-agriculture' would be.

If, however, we are discussing the 'purely economic' conditions of the epoch of finance capital as a historically concrete epoch which began at the turn of the twentieth century, then the best reply that one can make to the lifeless abstractions of 'ultra-imperialism' (which serve exclusively a most reactionary aim: that of diverting attention from the depth of *existing* antagonisms) is to contrast them with the concrete economic realities of the present-day world economy. Kautsky's utterly meaningless talk about ultra-imperialism encourages, among other things, that profoundly mistaken idea which only brings grist to the mill of the apologists of imperialism, i.e., that the rule of finance capital *lessens* the unevenness and contradictions inherent in the world economy, whereas in reality it *increases* them.

R. Calwer, in his little book, *An Introduction to the World Economy,*[5] made an attempt to summarize the main, purely economic, data that enable one to obtain a concrete picture of the internal relations of the world economy at the turn of the twentieth century. He divides the world into five 'main economic areas', as follows: (1) Central Europe (the whole of Europe with the exception of Russia and Great Britain); (2) Great Britain; (3) Russia; (4) Eastern Asia; (5) America; he includes the colonies in the 'areas' of the states to which they belong and 'leaves aside' a few countries not distributed according to areas, such as Persia, Afghanistan, and Arabia in Asia, Morocco and Abyssinia in Africa, etc.

Here is a brief summary of the economic data he quotes on these regions.

---

[5] R. Calwer, *Einführung in die Weltwirtschaft*, Berlin, 1906.

Principal Economic Areas	Area (m. sq. km.)	Pop. (m.)	Transport railways (000 km.)	Transport mercantile fleet (000 m. tons)	Trade imports, exports (marks)	Industry Output of coal (m. tons)	Industry Output of pig iron (m. tons)	Industry Output No. of cotton spindles (m.)
1) Central Europe	27.6 (23.6)*	388 (146)	204	8	41	251	15	26
2) Britain	28.9 (28.6)*	398 (355)	140	11	25	249	9	51
3) Russia	22	131	63	1	3	16	3	7
4) Eastern Asia	21	389	8	1	2	8	0.02	2
5) America	30	148	379	6	14	245	14	19

* The figures in parantheses show the area and population of the colonies.

We see three areas of highly developed capitalism (high development of means of transport, of trade and of industry): the Central European, the British and the American areas. Among these are three states which dominate the world: Germany, Great Britain, and the United States. Imperialist rivalry and the struggle between these countries have become extremely keen because Germany has only an insignificant area and few colonies; the creation of 'Central Europe' is still a matter for the future, it is being born in the midst of a desperate struggle. For the moment the distinctive feature of the whole of Europe is political disunity. In the British and American areas, on the other hand, political concentration is very highly developed, but there is a vast disparity between the immense colonies of the one and the insignificant colonies of the other. In the colonies, however, capitalism is only beginning to develop. The struggle for South America is becoming more and more acute.

There are two areas where capitalism is little developed: Russia and Eastern Asia. In the former, the population is extremely sparse, in the latter it is extremely dense; in the former political concentration is high, in the latter it does not exist. The partitioning of China is only just beginning, and the struggle for it between Japan, the US, etc., is continually gaining in intensity.

Compare this reality – the vast diversity of economic and political conditions, the extreme disparity in the rate of development of the various countries, etc., and the violent struggles among the imperialist states – with Kautsky's silly little fable about 'peaceful' ultra-imperialism. Is this not the reactionary attempt of a frightened philistine to hide from stern reality? Are not the international cartels which Kautsky imagines are the embryos of 'ultra-imperialism' (in the same way as one 'can' describe the manufacture of tablets in a laboratory as ultra-agriculture in embryo) an example of the division *and the redivision* of the world, the transition from peaceful division to non-peaceful division and vice-ersa? Is not American and other finance capital, which divided the whole world peacefully with Germany's participation in, for example, the international rail syndicate, or in the international mercantile shipping trust, now engaged in *redividing* the world on the basis of a new relation of forces that is being changed by methods *anything but* peaceful?

Finance capital and the trusts do not diminish but increase the differences in the rate of growth of the various parts of the world economy. Once the relation of forces is changed, what other solution of the contradictions can be found *under capitalism* than that of *force?* Railway statistics[6] provide remarkably exact data on the different rates of growth of capitalism and finance capital in world economy. In the last decades of imperialist development, the total length of railways has changed as follows:

RAILWAYS (*000 kilometres*)

	1890	1913	+
Europe	224	346	+122
US	268	411	+143
All colonies	82 ⎫ 125	210 ⎫ 347	+128 ⎫ +222
Independent and semi-independent states of Asia and America	43 ⎭	137 ⎭	+ 94 ⎭
Total	617	1,104	

Thus, the development of railways has been most rapid in the colonies and in the independent (and semi-independent) states of Asia and America. Here, as we know, the finance capital of the four or five biggest capitalist states holds undisputed sway. Two hundred thousand

---

[6] *Statistisches Jahrbuch für das deutsche Reich, 1915; Archiv für Eisenbahnwesen, 1892.* Minor details for the distribution of railways among the colonies of the various countries in 1890 had to be estimated approximately.

kilometres of new railways in the colonies and in the other countries of Asia and America represent a capital of more than 40,000 million marks newly invested on particularly advantageous terms, with special guarantees of a good return and with profitable orders for steel works, etc., etc.

Capitalism is growing with the greatest rapidity in the colonies and in overseas countries. Among the latter, *new* imperialist powers are emerging (e.g., Japan). The struggle among the world imperialisms is becoming more acute. The tribute levied by finance capital on the most profitable colonial and overseas enterprises is increasing. In the division of this 'booty', an exceptionally large part goes to countries which do not always stand at the top of the list in the rapidity of the development of their productive forces. In the case of the biggest countries, together with their colonies, the total length of railways was as follows:

RAILWAYS (*000 kilometres*)

	1890	1913	
US	268	413	+145
British Empire	107	208	+101
Russia	32	78	+ 46
Germany	43	68	+ 25
France	41	63	+ 22
Total for 5 powers	491	830	+339

Thus, about 80 per cent of the total existing railways are concentrated in the hands of the five biggest powers. But the concentration of the *ownership of* these railways, the concentration of finance capital, is immeasurably greater since the French and British millionaires, for example, own an enormous amount of shares and bonds in American, Russian and other railways.

Thanks to her colonies, Great Britain has increased the length of 'her' railways by 100,000 kilometres, four times as much as Germany. And yet, it is well known that the development of productive forces in Germany, and especially the development of the coal and iron industries, has been incomparably more rapid during this period than in Britain – not to speak of France and Russia. In 1892, Germany produced 4,900,000 tons of pig iron and Great Britain produced 6,800,000 tons; in 1912, Germany produced 17,600,000 tons and Great Britain, 9,000,000 tons. Germany, therefore, had an overwhelming superiority over Britain in this respect.[7] The question is: what means other than war could there be *under capitalism* to overcome the disparity between the development of productive forces and the accumulation of capital on the one side, and the division of colonies and spheres of influence for finance capital on the other?

[7] Cf. also Edgar Crammond, 'The Economic Relations of the British and German Empires' in *The Journal of the Royal Statistical Society*, July 1914, p. 777 et seq.

8

PARASITISM AND DECAY OF CAPITALISM

We now have
to examine yet another significant aspect of imperialism to which most of the discussions on the subject usually attach insufficient importance. One of the shortcomings of the Marxist Hilferding is that on this point he has taken a step backward compared with the non-Marxist Hobson. I refer to parasitism, which is characteristic of imperialism.

As we have seen, the deepest economic foundation of imperialism is monopoly. This is capitalist monopoly, i.e., monopoly which has grown out of capitalism and which exists in the general environment of capitalism, commodity production and competition, in permanent and insoluble contradiction to this general environment. Nevertheless, like all monopoly, it inevitably engenders a tendency of stagnation and decay. Since monopoly prices are established, even temporarily, the motive cause of technical and, consequently, of all other progress disappears to a certain extent and, further, the *economic* possibility arises of deliberately retarding technical progress. For instance, in America, a certain Owens invented a machine which revolutionized the manufacture of bottles. The German bottle-manufacturing cartel purchased Owens's patent, but pigeon-holed it, refrained from utilizing it. Certainly, monopoly under capitalism can never completely, and for a very long period of time, eliminate competition in the world market (and this, by the by, is one of the reasons why the theory of ultra-imperialism is so absurd). Certainly, the possibility of reducing the cost of production and increasing profits by introducing technical improvements operates in the direction of change. But the *tendency* to stagnation and decay, which is characteristic of monopoly, continues to operate, and in some branches of industry, in some countries, for certain periods of time, it gains the upper hand.

The monopoly ownership of very extensive, rich or well-situated colonies operates in the same direction.

Further, imperialism is an immense accumulation of money capital in a few countries, amounting, as we have seen, to 100,000–150,000 million francs in securities. Hence the extraordinary growth of a class, or rather, of a stratum of rentiers, i.e., people who live by 'clipping coupons', who take no part in any enterprise whatever, whose profession is idleness. The export of capital, one of the most essential economic bases of imperialism, still more completely isolates the rentiers from production and sets the seal of parasitism on the whole country that lives by exploiting the labour of several overseas countries and colonies.

'In 1893,' writes Hobson, 'the British capital invested abroad represented about 15 per cent of the total wealth of the United Kingdom.'[1] Let me remind the reader that by 1915 this capital had increased about two and a half times. 'Aggressive imperialism,' says Hobson further on, 'which costs the tax-payer so dear, which is of so little value to the manufacturer and trader . . . is a source of great gain to the investor. . . . The annual income Great Britain derives from commissions in her whole foreign and colonial trade, import and export, is estimated by Sir R. Giffen at £18,000,000 [nearly 170 million rubles] for 1899, taken at 2½ per cent, upon a turnover of £800,000,000.' Great as this sum is, it cannot explain the aggressive imperialism of Great Britain, which is explained by the income of £90 million to £100 million from 'invested' capital, the income of the rentiers.

The income of the rentiers is *five times greater* than the income obtained from the foreign trade of the biggest 'trading' country in the world! This is the essence of imperialism and imperialist parasitism.

---

[1] Hobson, op. cit., pp. 59, 62.

For that reason the term 'rentier state' (Rentnerstaat), or usurer state, is coming into common use in the economic literature that deals with imperialism. The world has become divided into a handful of usurer states and a vast majority of debtor states. At the top of the list of foreign investments,' says Schulze-Gaevernitz, 'are those placed in politically dependent or allied countries: Great Britain grants loans to Egypt, Japan, China and South America. Her navy plays here the part of bailiff in case of necessity. Great Britain's political power protects her from the indignation of her debtors.'[2] Sartorius von Waltershausen in his book, *The National Economic System of Capital Investments Abroad*, cites Holland as the model 'rentier state' and points out that Great Britain and France are now becoming such.[3] Schilder is of the opinion that five industrial states have become 'definitely pronounced creditor countries': Great Britain, France, Germany, Belgium and Switzerland. He does not include Holland in this list simply because she is 'industrially little developed'.[4] The United States is a creditor only of the American countries.

'Great Britain,' says Schulze-Gaevernitz, 'is gradually becoming transformed from an industrial into a creditor state. Notwithstanding the absolute increase in industrial output and the export of manufactured goods, there is an increase in the relative importance of income from interest and dividends, issues of securities, commissions and speculation in the whole of the national economy. In my opinion it is precisely this that forms the economic basis of imperialist ascendancy. The creditor is more firmly attached to the debtor than the seller is to the buyer.'[5] In regard to Germany, A. Lansburgh, the publisher of the Berlin *Die Bank*, in 1911, in an article entitled 'Germany – a Rentier State', wrote the following: 'People in Germany are ready to sneer at the yearning to become rentiers that is observed in France. But they forget that as far as the bourgeoisie is concerned the situation in Germany is becoming more and more like that in France.'[6]

The rentier state is a state of parasitic, decaying capitalism, and

---

[2] Schulze-Gaevernitz, *Britischer Imperialismus*, S, 320 et seq.
[3] Sartorius von Waltershausen. *Das volkswirtschaftliche System, etc*, Berlin, 1907, Buch IV.
[4] Schilder, op. cit., S. 393.
[5] Schulze-Gaevernitz, op. cit., S. 122.
[6] *Die Bank*, 1911, 1, S. 10–11.

this circumstance cannot fail to influence all the socio-political conditions of the countries concerned, in general, and the two fundamental trends in the working-class movement, in particular. To demonstrate this in the clearest possible manner let me quote Hobson, who is a most reliable witness, since he cannot be suspected of leaning towards Marxist orthodoxy; on the other hand, he is an Englishman who is very well acquainted with the situation in the country which is richest in colonies, in finance capital, and in imperialist experience.

With the Anglo–Boer War fresh in his mind, Hobson describes the connection between imperialism and the interests of the 'financiers', their growing profits from contracts, supplies, etc., and writes: 'While the directors of this definitely parasitic policy are capitalists, the same motives appeal to special classes of the workers. In many towns most important trades are dependent upon government employment or contracts; the imperialism of the metal and shipbuilding centres is attributable in no small degree to this fact.' Two sets of circumstances, in this writer's opinion, have weakened the old empires: (1) 'economic parasitism', and (2) the formation of armies recruited from subject peoples. 'There is first the habit of economic parasitism, by which the ruling state has used its provinces, colonies, and dependencies in order to enrich its ruling class and to bribe its lower classes into acquiescence.' And I shall add that the economic possibility of such bribery, whatever its form may be, requires high monopolist profits.

As for the second circumstance, Hobson writes: 'One of the strangest symptoms of the blindness of imperialism is the reckless indifference with which Great Britain, France and other imperial nations are embarking on this perilous dependence. Great Britain has gone farthest. Most of the fighting by which we have won our Indian Empire has been done by natives; in India, as more recently in Egypt, great standing armies are placed under British commanders; almost all the fighting associated with our African dominions, except in the southern part, has been done for us by natives.'

Hobson gives the following economic appraisal of the prospect of the partitioning of China: 'The greater part of Western Europe might then assume the appearance and character already exhibited by tracts of country in the South of England, in the Riviera and in the tourist-ridden or residential parts of Italy and Switzerland, little clusters of wealthy aristocrats drawing dividends and pensions from the Far East, with a somewhat larger group of professional retainers and tradesmen and a larger body of personal servants and workers in the transport trade and in the final stages of production of the more perishable goods; all the main arterial industries would have disappeared, the staple foods and manufactures flowing in as tribute from Asia and Africa. . . . We have foreshadowed the possibility of even a larger alliance of Western states, a European federation of great powers which, so far from forwarding the cause of world civilization, might introduce the gigantic peril of a Western parasitism, a group of advanced industrial nations, whose upper classes drew vast tribute from Asia and Africa, with which they supported great tame masses of retainers, no longer engaged in the staple industries of agriculture and manufacture, but kept in the performance of personal or minor industrial services under the control of a new financial aristocracy. Let those who would scout such a theory [it would be better to say: prospect] as undeserving of consideration examine the economic and social condition of districts in Southern England today which are already reduced to this condition, and reflect upon the vast extension of such a system which might be rendered feasible by the subjection of China to the economic control of similar groups of financiers, investors, and political and business officials, draining the greatest potential reservoir of profit the world has ever known, in order to consume it in Europe. The situation is far too complex, the play of world forces far too incalculable, to render this or any other single interpretation of the future very probable; but the influences which govern the imperialism of Western Europe today are moving in this direction, and, unless counteracted or diverted, make towards some such consummation.'[7]

The author is quite right: *if* the forces of imperialism had not been counteracted they would have led precisely to what he has described. The significance of a 'United States of Europe' in the present imperialist situation is correctly appraised. He should have added, however, that, also *within* the working-class movement, the opportunists, who are for the moment victorious in most countries, are 'working' systematically and un-deviatingly in this very direction. Imperialism, which means the partitioning of the world, and the exploitation of other countries besides

[7] Hobson, op, cit., pp. 103, 205, 144, 335, 386.

China, which means high monopoly profits for a handful of very rich countries, makes it economically possible to bribe the upper strata of the proletariat, and thereby fosters, gives shape to, and strengthens opportunism. We must not, however, lose sight of the forces which counteract imperialism in general, and opportunism in particular, and which, naturally, the social-liberal Hobson is unable to perceive.

The German opportunist, Gerhard Hildebrand, who was once expelled from the Party for defending imperialism, and who could today be a leader of the so-called 'Social-Democratic' Party of Germany, supplements Hobson well by his advocacy of a 'United States of Western Europe' (without Russia) for the purpose of 'joint' action . . . against the African Negroes, against the 'great Islamic movement', for the maintenance of a 'powerful army and navy', against a 'Sino–Japanese coalition',[8] etc.

The description of 'British imperialism' in Schulze-Gaevernitz's book reveals the same parasitical traits. The national income of Great Britain approximately doubled from 1865 to 1898, while the income 'from abroad' increased *ninefold* in the same period. While the 'merit' of imperialism is that it 'trains the Negro to habits of industry' (you cannot manage without coercion . . .), the 'danger' of imperialism lies in that 'Europe will shift the burden of physical toil – first agricultural and mining, then the rougher work in industry – on to the coloured races, and itself be content with the role of rentier, and in this way, perhaps, pave the way for the economic, and later, the political emancipation of the coloured races'.

An increasing proportion of land in England is being taken out of cultivation and used for sport, for the diversion of the rich. As far as Scotland – the most aristocratic place for hunting and other sports – is concerned, it is said that 'it lives on its past and on Mr Carnegie' (the American multimillionaire). On horse racing and fox hunting alone England annually spends £14,000,000 (nearly 130 million rubles). The number of rentiers in England is about one million. The percentage of the productively employed population to the total population is declining:

[8] Gerhard Hildebrand, *Die Erschütterung der Industrieherrschaft und des Industriesozialismus*, 1910, S. 229, et seq.

	Population England and Wales (000,000)	Workers in basic industries (000,000)	Per cent of total population
1851	17.9	4.1	23
1901	32.5	4.9	15

And in speaking of the British working class the bourgeois student of 'British imperialism at the beginning of the twentieth century' is obliged to distinguish systematically between the '*upper stratum*' of the workers and the '*lower stratum of the proletariat proper*'. The upper stratum furnishes the bulk of the membership of co-operatives, of trade unions, of sporting clubs and of numerous religious sects. To this level is adapted the electoral system, which in Great Britain is still '*sufficiently restricted to exclude the lower stratum of the proletariat proper*'! In order to present the condition of the British working class in a rosy light, only this upper stratum – which constitutes a *minority* of the proletariat – is usually spoken of. For instance, 'the problem of unemployment is mainly a London problem and that of the lower proletarian stratum, *to which the politicians attach little importance*. . . . '[9] He should have said: to which the bourgeois politicians and the 'socialist' opportunists attach little importance.

One of the special features of imperialism connected with the facts I am describing, is the decline in emigration from imperialist countries and the increase in immigration into these countries from the more backward countries where lower wages are paid. As Hobson observes, emigration from Great Britain has been declining since 1884. In that year the number of emigrants was 242,000, while in 1900, the number was 169,000. Emigration from Germany reached the highest point between 1881 and 1890, with a total of 1,453,000 emigrants. In the course of the following two decades, it fell to 544,000 and to 341,000. On the other hand, there was an increase in the number of workers entering Germany from Austria, Italy, Russia and other countries. According to the 1907 census, there were 1,342,294 foreigners in Germany, of whom 440,800 were industrial workers and 257,329 agricultural workers.[10] In France, the workers employed in the mining industry are, 'in great part', foreigners:

[9] Schulze-Gaeveraitz, *Britischer Imperialismus*, S, 301.
[10] *Statistik des Deutschen Reichs*, Bd. 211.

Poles, Italians and Spaniards.[11] In the United States, immigrants from Eastern and Southern Europe are engaged in the most poorly paid jobs, while American workers provide the highest percentage of overseers or of the better-paid workers.[12] Imperialism has the tendency to create privileged sections also among the workers, and to detach them from the broad masses of the proletariat.

It must be observed that in Great Britain the tendency of imperialism to split the workers, to strengthen opportunism among them and to cause temporary decay in the working-class movement, revealed itself much earlier than the end of the nineteenth and the beginning of the twentieth centuries; for two important distinguishing features of imperialism were already observed in Great Britain in the middle of the nineteenth century – vast colonial possessions and a monopolist position in the world market. Marx and Engels traced this connection between opportunism in the working-class movement and the imperialist features of British capitalism systematically, during the course of several decades. For example, on October 7, 1858, Engels wrote to Marx: 'The English proletariat is actually becoming more and more bourgeois, so that this most bourgeois of all nations is apparently aiming ultimately at the possession of a bourgeois aristocracy and a bourgeois proletariat *alongside* the bourgeoisie. For a nation which exploits the whole world this is of course to a certain extent justifiable.' Almost a quarter of a century later, in a letter dated August 11, 1881, Engels speaks of the 'worst English trade unions which allow themselves to be led by men sold to, or at least paid by, the middle class'. In a letter to Kautsky, dated September 12, 1882, Engels wrote: 'You ask me what the English workers think about colonial policy. Well, exactly the same as they think about politics in general. There is no workers' party here, there are only Conservatives and Liberal-Radicals, and the workers gaily share the feast of England's monopoly of the world market and the colonies.'[13] (Engels expressed similar ideas in the press in his preface to the second edition of *The Condition of the Working Class in England*, which appeared in 1892.)

---

[11] Henger, *Die Kapitalsanlage der Franzosen*, Stuttgart, 1913.

[12] Hourwich, *Immigration and Labour*, New York, 1913.

[13] *Briefwechsel von Marx und Engels*, Bd. II, S. 290; IV, 433. – Karl Kautsky, *Sozialismus und Kolonialpolitik*, Berlin, 1907, S. 79; this pamphlet was written by Kautsky in those infinitely distant days when he was still a Marxist.

This clearly shows the causes and effects. The causes are: (1) exploitation of the whole world by this country; (2) its monopolist position in the world market; (3) its colonial monopoly. The effects are: (1) a section of the British proletariat becomes bourgeois; (2) a section of the proletariat allows itself to be led by men bought by, or at least paid by, the bourgeoisie. The imperialism of the beginning of the twentieth century completed the division of the world among a handful of states, each of which today exploits (in the sense of drawing superprofits from) a part of the 'whole world' only a little smaller than that which England exploited in 1858; each of them occupies a monopolist position in the world market thanks to trusts, cartels, finance capital and creditor and debtor relations; each of them enjoys to some degree a colonial monopoly (we have seen that out of the total of 75,000,000 sq. km., which comprise the *whole* colonial world, *65,000,000* sq. km., or 86 per cent, belong to six powers; *61,000,000* sq. km., or 81 per cent, belong to three powers).

The distinctive feature of the present situation is the prevalence of such economic and political conditions that are bound to increase the irreconcilability between opportunism and the general and vital interests of the working-class movement: imperialism has grown from an embryo into the predominant system; capitalist monopolies occupy first place in economics and politics; the division of the world has been completed; on the other hand, instead of the undivided monopoly of Great Britain, we see a few imperialist powers contending for the right to share in this monopoly, and this struggle is characteristic of the whole period of the early twentieth century. Opportunism cannot now be completely triumphant in the working-class movement of one country for decades as it was in Britain in the second half of the nineteenth century; but in a number of countries it has grown ripe, overripe, and rotten, and has become completely merged with bourgeois policy in the form of 'social-chauvinism'.[14]

---

[14] Russian social-chauvinism in its overt form, represented by the Potresovs, Chkhenkelis, Maslovs, etc., and in its covert form (Chkheidze, Skobelev, Axelrod, Martov, etc.), also emerged from the Russian variety of opportunism, namely, liquidationism.

9

CRITIQUE OF IMPERIALISM

By the critique
of imperialism, in the broad sense of the term, we mean the attitude of the different classes of society towards imperialist policy in connection with their general ideology.

The enormous dimensions of finance capital concentrated in a few hands and creating an extraordinarily dense and widespread network of relationships and connections which subordinates not only the small and medium, but also the very small capitalists and small masters, on the one hand, and the increasingly intense struggle waged against other national state groups of financiers for the division of the world and domination over other countries, on the other hand, cause the propertied classes to go over entirely to the side of imperialism. 'General' enthusiasm over the prospects of imperialism, furious defence of it and painting it in the brightest colours – such are the signs of the times. Imperialist ideology also penetrates the working class. No Chinese Wall separates it from the other classes. The leaders of the present-day, so-called, 'Social-Democratic' Party of Germany are justly called 'social-imperialists', that is, socialists in words and imperialists in deeds; but as early as 1902, Hobson noted the existence in Britain of 'Fabian imperialists' who belonged to the opportunist Fabian Society.

Bourgeois scholars and publicists usually come out in defence of imperialism in a somewhat veiled form; they obscure its complete domination and its deep-going roots, strive to push specific and secondary details into the forefront and do their very best to distract attention from essentials by means of absolutely ridiculous schemes for 'reform', such as police supervision of the trusts or banks, etc. Cynical and frank imperialists who are bold enough to admit the absurdity of the idea of reforming the fundamental characteristics of imperialism are a rarer phenomenon.

Here is an example. The German imperialists attempt, in the magazine *Archives of World Economy,* to follow the national emancipation movements in the colonies, particularly, of course, in colonies other than those belonging to Germany. They note the unrest and the protest movements in India, the movement in Natal (South Africa), in the Dutch East Indies, etc. One of them, commenting on an English report of a conference held on June 28–30, 1910, of representatives of various subject nations and races, of peoples of Asia, Africa and Europe who are under foreign rule, writes as follows in appraising the speeches delivered at this conference: 'We are told that we must fight imperialism; that the ruling states should recognize the right of subject peoples to independence; that an international tribunal should supervise the fulfilment of treaties concluded between the great powers and weak peoples. Further than the expression of these pious wishes they do not go. We see no trace of understanding of the fact that imperialism is inseparably bound up with capitalism in its present form and that, therefore [!!], an open struggle against imperialism would be hopeless, unless, perhaps, the fight were to be confined to protests against certain of its especially abhorrent excesses.'[1] Since the reform of the basis of imperialism is a deception, a 'pious wish', since the bourgeois representatives of the oppressed nations go no 'further' forward, the bourgeois representative of an oppressing nation goes 'further' *backward,* to servility towards imperialism under cover of the claim to be 'scientific'. That is also 'logic'!

The questions as to whether it is possible to reform the basis of imperialism, whether to go forward to the further intensification and

---

[1] *Weltwirtschaftishes Archiv,* Bd. II, S. 193.

deepening of the antagonisms which it engenders, or backward, towards allaying these antagonisms, are fundamental questions in the critique of imperialism. Since the specific political features of imperialism are reaction everywhere and increased national oppression due to the oppression of the financial oligarchy and the elimination of free competition, a petty-bourgeois-democratic opposition to imperialism arose at the beginning of the twentieth century in nearly all imperialist countries. Kautsky not only did not trouble to oppose, was not only unable to oppose this petty-bourgeois reformist opposition, which is really reactionary in its economic basis, but became merged with it in practice, and this is precisely where Kautsky and the broad international Kautskian trend deserted Marxism.

In the United States, the imperialist war waged against Spain in 1898 stirred up the opposition of the 'anti-imperialists', the last of the Mohicans of bourgeois democracy who declared this war to be 'criminal', regarded the annexation of foreign territories as a violation of the Constitution, declared that the treatment of Aguinaldo, leader of the Filipinos (the Americans promised him the independence of his country, but later landed troops and annexed it), was 'Jingo treachery', and quoted the words of Lincoln: 'When the white man governs himself, that is self-government; but when he governs himself and also governs others, it is no longer self-government; it is despotism.'[2] But as long as all this criticism shrank from recognizing the inseverable bond between imperialism and the trusts, and, therefore, between imperialism and the foundations of capitalism, while it shrank from joining the forces engendered by large-scale capitalism and its development – it remained a 'pious wish'.

This is also the main attitude taken by Hobson in his critique of imperialism. Hobson anticipated Kautsky in protesting against the 'inevitability of imperialism' argument, and in urging the necessity of 'increasing the consuming capacity' of the people (under capitalism!). The petty-bourgeois point of view in the critique of imperialism, the omnipotence of the banks, the financial oligarchy, etc., is adopted by the authors I have often quoted, such as Agahd, A. Lansburgh, L. Eschwege, and among the French writers Victor Berard, author of a superficial book entitled *England and Imperialism* which appeared in 1900. All these authors, who

---

[2] J. Patouillet, *L'impérialisme américain*, Dijon, 1904, p. 272.

make no claim to be Marxists, contrast imperialism with free competition and democracy, condemn the Baghdad railway scheme, which is leading to conflicts and war, utter 'pious wishes' for peace, etc. This applies also to the compiler of international stock and share issue statistics, A. Neymarck, who, after calculating the thousands of millions of francs representing 'international' securities, exclaimed in 1912: 'Is it possible to believe that peace may be disturbed . . . that, in the face of these enormous figures, anyone would risk starting a war?'[3]

Such simple-mindedness on the part of the bourgeois economists is not surprising; moreover, *it is in their interest* to pretend to be so naive and to talk 'seriously' about peace under imperialism. But what remains of Kautsky's Marxism, when, in 1914, 1915 and 1916, he takes up the same bourgeois-reformist point of view and affirms that 'everybody is agreed' (imperialists, pseudo-socialists and social-pacifists) on the matter of peace? Instead of an analysis of imperialism and an exposure of the depths of its contradictions, we have nothing but a reformist 'pious wish' to wave them aside, to evade them.

Here is a sample of Kautsky's economic criticism of imperialism. He takes the statistics of the British export and import trade with Egypt for 1872 and 1912; it seems that this export and import trade has grown more slowly than British foreign trade as a whole. From this Kautsky concludes that 'we have no reason to suppose that without military occupation the growth of British trade with Egypt would have been less, simply as a result of the mere operation of economic factors'. 'The urge of capital to expand . . . can be best promoted, not by the violent methods of imperialism, but by peaceful democracy.'[4]

This argument of Kautsky's, which is repeated in every key by his Russian armour-bearer (and Russian shielder of the social-chauvinists), Mr. Spectator, constitutes the basis of Kautskian critique of imperialism, and that is why we must deal with it in greater detail. We will begin with a quotation from Hilferding, whose conclusions Kautsky on many occasions, and notably in April 1915, has declared to have been 'unanimously adopted by all socialist theoreticians'.

---

[3] *Bulletin de l'Institut International de Statistique*, T. XIX, livr. II, p. 225.
[4] Kautsky, *Nationalstaat, imperialistischer Staat und Staatenbund*, Nürnberg, 1915, S. 72, 70.

'It is not the business of the proletariat,' writes Hilferding, 'to contrast the more progressive capitalist policy with that of the now bygone era of free trade and of hostility towards the state. The reply of the proletariat to the economic policy of finance capital, to imperialism, cannot be free trade, but socialism. The aim of proletarian policy cannot today be the ideal of restoring free competition – which has now become a reactionary ideal – but the complete elimination of competition by the abolition of capitalism.'[5]

Kautsky broke with Marxism by advocating in the epoch of finance capital a 'reactionary ideal', 'peaceful democracy', 'the mere operation of economic factors', for *objectively* this ideal drags us back from monopoly to non-monopoly capitalism, and is a reformist swindle.

Trade with Egypt (or with any other colony or semi-colony) 'would have grown more' *without* military occupation, without imperialism, and without finance capital. What does this mean? That capitalism would have developed more rapidly if free competition had not been restricted by monopolies in general, or by the 'connections', yoke (i.e., also the monopoly) of finance capital, or by the monopolist possession of colonies by certain countries?

Kautsky's argument can have no other meaning; and *this* 'meaning' is meaningless. Let us assume that free competition, without any sort of monopoly, *would* have developed capitalism and trade more rapidly. But the more rapidly trade and capitalism develop, the greater is the concentration of production and capital which *gives rise* to monopoly. And monopolies have *already* arisen – precisely *out of* free competition! Even if monopolies have now begun to retard progress, it is not an argument in favour of free competition, which has become impossible after it has given rise to monopoly.

Whichever way one turns Kautsky's argument, one will find nothing in it except reaction and bourgeois reformism.

Even if we correct this argument and say, as Spectator says, that the trade of the colonies with Britain is now developing more slowly than their trade with other countries, it does not save Kautsky; for it is *also* monopoly, *also* imperialism that is beating Great Britain, only it is the monopoly and imperialism of another country (America, Germany). It is

---

[5] *Finance Capital*, p. 567.

known that the cartels have given rise to a new and peculiar form of protective tariffs, i.e., goods suitable for export are protected (Engels noted this in Vol. III of *Capital* [Marx, *Capital*, volume III, Moscow: Progress Publishers, 1971, p. 120]). It is known, too, that the cartels and finance capital have a system peculiar to themselves, that of 'exporting goods at cut-rate prices', or 'dumping', as the English call it: within a given country the cartel sells its goods at high monopoly prices, but sells them abroad at a much lower price to undercut the competitor, to enlarge its own production to the utmost, etc. If Germany's trade with the British colonies is developing more rapidly than Great Britain's, it only proves that German imperialism is younger, stronger and better organized than British imperialism, is superior to it; but it by no means proves the 'superiority' of free trade, for it is not a fight between free trade and protection and colonial dependence, but between two rival imperialisms, two monopolies, two groups of finance capital. The superiority of German imperialism over British imperialism is more potent than the wall of colonial frontiers or of protective tariffs: to use this as an 'argument' *in favour* of free trade and 'peaceful democracy' is banal, it means forgetting the essential features and characteristics of imperialism, substituting petty-bourgeois reformism for Marxism.

It is interesting to note that even the bourgeois economist, A. Lansburgh, whose criticism of imperialism is as petty-bourgeois as Kautsky's, nevertheless got closer to a more scientific study of trade statistics. He did not compare one single country, chosen at random, and one single colony with the other countries; he examined the export trade of an imperialist country: (1) with countries which are financially dependent upon it, and borrow money from it; and (2) with countries which are financially independent. He obtained the following results:

EXPORT TRADE OF GERMANY (*000,000 marks*)

		1889	1908	Per cent increase
	Rumania	48.2	70.8	47
To countries	Portugal	19.0	32.8	73
financially	Argentina	60.7	147.0	143
dependent on	Brazil	48.7	84.5	73
Germany	Chile	28.3	52.4	85
	Turkey	29.9	64.0	114
	Total	*234.8*	*451.5*	*92*

EXPORT TRADE OF GERMANY (*000,000 marks*)

		1889	1908	Per cent increase
	Great Britain	651.8	997.4	53
To countries	France	210.2	437.9	108
financially	Belgium	137.2	322.8	135
independent of	Switzerland	177.4	401.1	127
Germany	Australia	21.2	64.5	205
	Dutch East Indies	8.8	40.7	363
	Total	*1,206.6*	*2,264.4*	*87*

Lansburgh did not draw *conclusions* and therefore, strangely enough, failed to observe that *if* the figures prove anything at all, they prove that *he is wrong*, for the exports to countries financially dependent on Germany have grown *more rapidly*, if only slightly, than exports to the countries which are financially independent (I emphasize the 'if', for Lansburgh's figures are far from complete.)

Tracing the connection between exports and loans, Lansburgh writes:

'In 1890–91, a Rumanian loan was floated through the German banks, which had already in previous years made advances on this loan. It was used chiefly to purchase railway materials in Germany. In 1891, German exports to Rumania amounted to 55 million marks. The following year they dropped to 39.4 million marks and, with fluctuations, to 25.4 million in 1900. Only in very recent years have they regained the level of 1891, thanks to two new loans.

'German exports to Portugal rose, following the loans of 1888–89, to 21,100,000 (1890); then, in the two following years, they dropped to 16,200,000 and 7,400,000, and regained their former level only in 1903.

'The figures of German trade with Argentina are still more striking. Loans were floated in 1888 and 1890; German exports to Argentina reached 60,700,000 marks (1889). Two years later they amounted to only 18,600,000 marks, less than one-third of the previous figure. It was not until 1901 that they regained and surpassed the level of 1889, and then only as a result of new loans floated by the state and by municipalities, with advances to build power stations, and with other credit operations.

'Exports to Chile, as a consequence of the loan of 1889, rose to 45,200,000 marks (in 1892), and a year later dropped to 22,500,000 marks.

A new Chilean loan floated by the German banks in 1906 was followed by a rise of exports to 84,700,000 marks in 1907, only to fall again to 52,400,000 marks in 1908.'[6]

From these facts Lansburgh draws the amusing petty-bourgeois moral of how unstable and irregular export trade is when it is bound up with loans, how bad it is to invest capital abroad instead of 'naturally' and 'harmoniously' developing home industry, how 'costly' are the millions in bakshish that Krupp has to pay in floating foreign loans, etc. But the facts tell us clearly: the increase in exports is connected with *just these* swindling tricks of finance capital, which is not concerned with bourgeois morality, but with skinning the ox twice – first, it pockets the profits from the loan; then it pockets other profits from the *same* loan which the borrower uses to make purchases from Krupp, or to purchase railway material from the Steel Syndicate, etc.

I repeat that I do not by any means consider Lansburgh's figures to be perfect; but I had to quote them because they are more scientific than Kautsky's and Spectator's and because Lansburgh showed the correct way to approach the question. In discussing the significance of finance capital in regard to exports, etc., one must be able to single out the connection of exports especially and solely with the tricks of the financiers, especially and solely with the sale of goods by cartels, etc. Simply to compare colonies with non-colonies, one imperialism with another imperialism, one semi-colony or colony (Egypt) with all other countries, is to evade and to obscure the very *essence* of the question.

Kautsky's theoretical critique of imperialism has nothing in common with Marxism and serves only as a preamble to propaganda for peace and unity with the opportunists and the social-chauvinists, precisely for the reason that it evades and obscures the very profound and fundamental contradictions of imperialism: the contradictions between monopoly and free competition which exists side by side with it, between the gigantic 'operations' (and gigantic profits) of finance capital and 'honest' trade in the free market, the contradiction between cartels and trusts, on the one hand, and non-cartelized industry, on the other, etc.

The notorious theory of 'ultra-imperialism', invented by Kautsky,

---

[6] *Die Bank*, 1909, 2, S. 819 et seq.

is just as reactionary. Compare his arguments on this subject in 1915, with Hobson's arguments in 1902.

Kautsky: '... Cannot the present imperialist policy be supplanted by a new, ultra-imperialist policy, which will introduce the joint exploitation of the world by internationally united finance capital in place of the mutual rivalries of national finance capitals? Such a new phase of capitalism is at any rate conceivable. Can it be achieved? Sufficient premises are still lacking to enable us to answer this question.'[7]

Hobson: 'Christendom thus laid out in a few great federal empires, each with a retinue of uncivilized dependencies, seems to many the most legitimate development of present tendencies, and one which would offer the best hope of permanent peace on an assured basis of inter-Imperialism.'

Kautsky called ultra-imperialism or super-imperialism what Hobson, thirteen years earlier, described as inter-imperialism. Except for coining a new and clever catchword, replacing one Latin prefix by another, the only progress Kautsky has made in the sphere of 'scientific' thought is that he gave out as Marxism what Hobson, in effect, described as the cant of English parsons. After the Anglo–Boer War it was quite natural for this highly honourable caste to exert their main efforts to *console* the British middle class and the workers who had lost many of their relatives on the battlefields of South Africa and who were obliged to pay higher taxes in order to guarantee still higher profits for the British financiers. And what better consolation could there be than the theory that imperialism is not so bad; that it stands close to inter- (or ultra-) imperialism, which can ensure permanent peace? No matter what the good intentions of the English parsons, or of sentimental Kautsky, may have been, the only objective, i.e., real, social significance of Kautsky's 'theory' is this: it is a most reactionary method of consoling the masses with hopes of permanent peace being possible under capitalism, by distracting their attention from the sharp antagonisms and acute problems of the present times, and directing it towards illusory prospects of an imaginary 'ultra-imperialism' of the future. Deception of the masses – that is all there is in Kautsky's 'Marxist' theory.

Indeed, it is enough to compare well-known and indisputable facts to become convinced of the utter falsity of the prospects which Kautsky tries to conjure up before the German workers (and the workers

---

[7] *Die Neue Zeit*, April 30, 1915, S. 144.

of all lands). Let us consider India, Indo-China and China. It is known that these three colonial and semi-colonial countries, with a population of six to seven hundred million, are subjected to the exploitation of the finance capital of several imperialist powers: Great Britain, France, Japan, the USA, etc. Let us assume that these imperialist countries form alliances against one another in order to protect or enlarge their possessions, their interests and their spheres of influence in these Asiatic states; these alliances will be 'inter-imperialist', or 'ultra-imperialist' alliances. Let us assume that *all* the imperialist countries conclude an alliance for the 'peaceful' division of these parts of Asia; this alliance would be an alliance of 'internationally united finance capital'. There are actual examples of alliances of this kind in the history of the twentieth century – the attitude of the powers to China, for instance. We ask, is it 'conceivable', assuming that the capitalist system remains intact – and this is precisely the assumption that Kautsky does make – that such alliances would be more than temporary, that they would eliminate friction, conflicts and struggle in every possible form?

The question has only to be presented clearly for any other than a negative answer to be impossible. This is because the only conceivable basis under capitalism for the division of spheres of influence, interests, colonies, etc., is a calculation of the *strength* of those participating, their general economic, financial, military strength, etc. And the strength of these participants in the division does not change to an equal degree, for the *even* development of different undertakings, trusts, branches of industry, or countries is impossible under capitalism. Half a century ago Germany was a miserable, insignificant country, if her capitalist strength is compared with that of the Britain of that time; Japan compared with Russia in the same way. Is it 'conceivable' that in ten or twenty years' time the relative strength of the imperialist powers will have remained unchanged? It is out of the question.

Therefore, in the realities of the capitalist system, and not in the banal philistine fantasies of English parsons, or of the German 'Marxist', Kautsky, 'inter-imperialist' or 'ultra-imperialist' alliances, no matter what form they may assume, whether of one imperialist coalition against another, or of a general alliance embracing *all* the imperialist powers, are *inevitably* nothing more than a 'truce' in periods between wars. Peaceful alliances prepare the ground for wars, and in their turn grow out of wars; the one conditions the other, producing alternating forms of peaceful and non-peaceful struggle on *one and the same* basis of imperialist connections and relations within world economics and world politics. But in order to pacify the workers and reconcile them with the social-chauvinists who have deserted to the side of the bourgeoisie, over-wise Kautsky *separates* one link of a single chain from another, separates the present peaceful (and ultra-imperialist, nay, ultra-ultra-imperialist) alliance of *all* the powers for the 'pacification' of China (remember the suppression of the Boxer Rebellion) from the non-peaceful conflict of tomorrow, which will prepare the ground for another 'peaceful' general alliance for the partition, say, of Turkey, on the day after tomorrow, *etc., etc.,* Instead of showing the living connection between periods of imperialist peace and periods of imperialist war, Kautsky presents the workers with a lifeless abstraction in order to reconcile them to their lifeless leaders.

An American writer, Hill, in his *A History of the Diplomacy in the International Development of Europe* refers in his preface to the following periods in the recent history of diplomacy: (1) the era of revolution; (2) the constitutional movement; (3) the present era of 'commercial imperialism'.[8] Another writer divides the history of Great Britain's 'world policy' since 1870 into four periods: (1) the first Asiatic period (that of the struggle against Russia's advance in Central Asia towards India); (2) the African period (approximately 1885–1902): that of the struggle against France for the partition of Africa (the 'Fashoda incident' of 1898 which brought her within a hair's breadth of war with France); (3) the second Asiatic period (alliance with Japan against Russia); and (4) the 'European' period, chiefly anti-German.[9] 'The political patrol clashes take place on the financial field,' wrote the banker, Riesser, in 1905, in showing how French finance capital operating in Italy was preparing the way for a political alliance of these countries, and how a conflict was developing between Germany and Great Britain over Persia, between all the European capitalists over Chinese loans, etc. Behold, the living reality of peaceful 'ultra-imperialist' alliances in their inseverable connection with ordinary imperialist conflicts!

Kautsky's obscuring of the deepest contradictions of imperialism, which inevitably boils down to painting imperialism in bright colours,

---

[8] David Jayne Hill, *A History of the Diplomacy in the International Development of Europe*, Vol. I, p. X.

[9] Schilder, op. cit, S. 178.

leaves its traces in this writer's criticism of the political features of imperialism. Imperialism is the epoch of finance capital and of monopolies, which introduce everywhere the striving for domination, not for freedom. Whatever the political system, the result of these tendencies is everywhere reaction and an extreme intensification of antagonisms in this field. Particularly intensified become the yoke of national oppression and the striving for annexations, i.e., the violation of national independence (for annexation is nothing but the violation of the right of nations to self-determination). Hilferding rightly notes the connection between imperialism and the intensification of national oppression. 'In the newly opened-up countries,' he writes, 'the capital imported into them intensifies antagonisms and excites against the intruders the constantly growing resistance of the peoples who are awakening to national consciousness; this resistance can easily develop into dangerous measures against foreign capital. The old social relations become completely revolutionized, the age-long agrarian isolation of "nations without history" is destroyed and they are drawn into the capitalist whirlpool. Capitalism itself gradually provides the subjugated with the means and resources for their emancipation and they set out to achieve the goal which once seemed highest to the European nations: the creation of a united national state as a means to economic and cultural freedom. This movement for national independence threatens European capital in its most valuable and most promising fields of exploitation, and European capital can maintain its domination only by continually increasing its military forces.'[10]

To this must be added that it is not only in newly opened-up countries, but also in the old, that imperialism is leading to annexation, to increased national oppression, and, consequently, also to increasing resistance. While objecting to the intensification of political reaction by imperialism, Kautsky leaves in the shade a question that has become particularly urgent, viz., the impossibility of unity with the opportunists in the epoch of imperialism. While objecting to annexations, he presents his objections in a form that is most acceptable and least offensive to the opportunists. He addresses himself to a German audience, yet he obscures the most topical and important point, for instance, the annexation of Alsace-Lorraine by Germany. In order to appraise this 'mental aberration'

---

[10] *Finance Capital*, p. 487.

of Kautsky's I shall take the following example. Let us suppose that a Japanese condemns the annexation of the Philippines by the Americans. The question is: will many believe that he does so because he has a horror of annexations as such, and not because he himself has a desire to annex the Philippines? And shall we not be constrained to admit that the 'fight' the Japanese is waging against annexations can be regarded as being sincere and politically honest only if he fights against the annexation of Korea by Japan, and urges freedom for Korea to secede from Japan?

Kautsky's theoretical analysis of imperialism, as well as his economic and political critique of imperialism, are permeated *through and through* with a spirit, absolutely irreconcilable with Marxism, of obscuring and glossing over the fundamental contradictions of imperialism and with a striving to preserve at all costs the crumbling unity with opportunism in the European working-class movement.

10 THE PLACE OF IMPERIALISM IN HISTORY

We have seen
that in its economic essence imperialism is monopoly capitalism. This in itself determines its place in history, for monopoly that grows out of the soil of free competition, and precisely out of free competition, is the transition from the capitalist system to a higher socio-economic order. We must take special note of the four principal types of monopoly, or principal manifestations of monopoly capitalism, which are characteristic of the epoch we are examining.

Firstly, monopoly arose out of the concentration of production at a very high stage. This refers to the monopolist capitalist associations, cartels, syndicates and trusts. We have seen the important part these play in present-day economic life. At the beginning of the twentieth century, monopolies had acquired complete supremacy in the advanced countries, and although the first steps towards the formation of the cartels were taken by countries enjoying the protection of high tariffs (Germany, America), Great Britain, with her system of free trade, revealed the same basic phenomenon, only a little later, namely, the birth of monopoly out of the concentration of production.

Secondly, monopolies have stimulated the seizure of the most important sources of raw materials, especially for the basic and most highly cartelized industries in capitalist society: the coal and iron industries. The monopoly of the most important sources of raw materials has enormously increased the power of big capital, and has sharpened the antagonism between cartelized and non-cartelized industry.

Thirdly, monopoly has sprung from the banks. The banks have developed from modest middleman enterprises into the monopolists of finance capital. Some three to five of the biggest banks in each of the foremost capitalist countries have achieved the 'personal link-up' between industrial and bank capital, and have concentrated in their hands the control of thousands upon thousands of millions which form the greater part of the capital and income of entire countries. A financial oligarchy, which throws a close network of dependence relationships over all the economic and political institutions of present-day bourgeois society without exception – such is the most striking manifestation of this monopoly.

Fourthly, monopoly has grown out of colonial policy. To the numerous 'old' motives of colonial policy, finance capital has added the struggle for the sources of raw materials, for the export of capital, for spheres of influence, i.e., for spheres for profitable deals, concessions, monopoly profits and so on, economic territory in general. When the colonies of the European powers, for instance, comprised only one-tenth of the territory of Africa (as was the case in 1876), colonial policy was able to develop by methods other than those of monopoly – by the 'free grabbing' of territories, so to speak. But when nine-tenths of Africa had been seized (by 1900), when the whole world had been divided up, there was inevitably ushered in the era of monopoly possession of colonies and, consequently, of particularly intense struggle for the division and the redivision of the world.

The extent to which monopolist capital has intensified all the contradictions of capitalism is generally known. It is sufficient to mention the high cost of living and the tyranny of the cartels. This intensification of contradictions constitutes the most powerful driving force of the transitional period of history, which began from the time of the final victory of world finance capital.

Monopolies, oligarchy, the striving for domination and not for freedom, the exploitation of an increasing number of small or weak nations by a handful of the richest or most powerful nations – all these have given birth to those distinctive characteristics of imperialism which compel us to define it as parasitic or decaying capitalism. More and more prominently there emerges, as one of the tendencies of imperialism, the creation of the 'rentier state', the usurer state, in which the bourgeoisie to an ever-increasing degree lives on the proceeds of capital exports and by 'clipping coupons'. It would be a mistake to believe that this tendency to decay precludes the rapid growth of capitalism. It does not. In the epoch of imperialism, certain branches of industry, certain strata of the bourgeoisie and certain countries betray, to a greater or lesser degree, now one and now another of these tendencies. On the whole, capitalism is growing far more rapidly than before; but this growth is not only becoming more and more uneven in general, its unevenness also manifests itself, in particular, in the decay of the countries which are richest in capital (Britain).

In regard to the rapidity of Germany's economic development, Riesser, the author of the book on the big German banks, states: 'The progress of the preceding period (1848–70), which had not been exactly slow, compares with the rapidity with which the whole of Germany's national economy, and with it German banking, progressed during this period (1870–1905) in about the same way as the speed of the mail coach in the good old days compares with the speed of the present-day automobile . . . which is whizzing past so fast that it endangers not only innocent pedestrians in its path, but also the occupants of the car.' In its turn, this finance capital which has grown with such extraordinary rapidity is not unwilling, precisely because it has grown so quickly, to pass on to a more 'tranquil' possession of colonies which have to be seized – and not only by peaceful methods – from richer nations. In the United States, economic development in the last decades has been even more rapid than in Germany, *and for this very reason*, the parasitic features of modern American capitalism have stood out with particular prominence. On the other hand, a comparison of, say, the republican American bourgeoisie with the monarchist Japanese or German bourgeoisie shows that the most pronounced political distinction diminishes to an extreme degree in the epoch of imperialism – not because it is unimportant in general, but because in all these cases we are talking about a bourgeoisie which has definite features of parasitism.

The receipt of high monopoly profits by the capitalists in one of the numerous branches of industry, in one of the numerous countries, etc., makes it economically possible for them to bribe certain sections of the workers, and for a time a fairly considerable minority of them, and win them to the side of the bourgeoisie of a given industry or given nation against all the others. The intensification of antagonisms between imperialist nations for the division of the world increases this urge. And so there is created that bond between imperialism and opportunism, which revealed itself first and most clearly in Great Britain, owing to the fact that certain features of imperialist development were observable there much earlier than in other countries. Some writers, L. Martov, for example, are prone to wave aside the connection between imperialism and opportunism in the working-class movement – a particularly glaring fact at the present time – by resorting to 'official optimism' (*à la* Kautsky and Huysmans) like the following: the cause of the opponents of capitalism would be hopeless if it were progressive capitalism that led to the increase of opportunism, or, if it were the best-paid workers who were inclined towards opportunism, etc. We must have no illusions about 'optimism' of this kind. It is optimism in respect of opportunism; it is optimism which serves to conceal opportunism. As a matter of fact the extraordinary rapidity and the particularly revolting character of the development of opportunism is by no means a guarantee that its victory will be durable: the rapid growth of a painful abscess on a healthy body can only cause it to burst more quickly and thus relieve the body of it. The most dangerous of all in this respect are those who do not wish to understand that the fight against imperialism is a sham and humbug unless it is inseparably bound up with the fight against opportunism.

From all that has been said in this book on the economic essence of imperialism, it follows that we must define it as capitalism in transition, or, more precisely, as moribund capitalism. It is very instructive in this respect to note that bourgeois economists, in describing modern capitalism, frequently employ catchwords and phrases like 'interlocking', 'absence of isolation', etc.; 'in conformity with their functions and course of development', banks are 'not purely private business enterprises; they are more and more outgrowing the sphere of purely private business regulation'. And this very Riesser, whose words I have just quoted, declares with all seriousness that the 'prophecy' of the Marxists concerning 'socialization' has 'not come true'!

What then does this catchword 'interlocking' express? It merely expresses the most striking feature of the process going on before our eyes. It shows that the observer counts the separate trees, but cannot see the wood. It slavishly copies the superficial, the fortuitous, the chaotic. It reveals the observer as one who is overwhelmed by the mass of raw material and is utterly incapable of appreciating its meaning and importance. Ownership of shares, the relations between owners of private property 'interlock in a haphazard way'. But underlying this interlocking, its very base, are the changing social relations of production. When a big enterprise assumes gigantic proportions, and, on the basis of an exact computation of mass data, organizes according to plan the supply of primary raw materials to the extent of two-thirds, or three-fourths, of all that is necessary for tens of millions of people; when the raw materials are transported in a systematic and organized manner to the most suitable places of production, sometimes situated hundreds or thousands of miles from each other; when a single centre directs all the consecutive stages of processing the material right up to the manufacture of numerous varieties of finished articles; when these products are distributed according to a single plan among tens and hundreds of millions of consumers (the marketing of oil in America and Germany by the American oil trust) – then it becomes evident that we have socialization of production, and not mere 'interlocking'; that private economic and private property relations constitute a shell which no longer fits its contents, a shell which must inevitably decay if its removal is artificially delayed, a shell which may remain in a state of decay for a fairly long period (if, at the worst, the cure of the opportunist abscess is protracted), but which will inevitably be removed.

The enthusiastic admirer of German imperialism, Schulze-Gaevernitz, exclaims:

'Once the supreme management of the German banks has been entrusted to the hands of a dozen persons, their activity is even today more significant for the public good than that of the majority of the Ministers of State. . . . [The 'interlocking' of bankers, ministers, magnates of industry and rentiers is here conveniently forgotten.] If we imagine the development of those tendencies we have noted carried to their logical conclusion we will have: the money capital of the nation united in the banks; the banks themselves combined into cartels; the investment capital of the nation cast in the shape of securities. Then the forecast of that genius

Saint-Simon will be fulfilled: 'The present anarchy of production, which corresponds to the fact that economic relations are developing without uniform regulation, must make way for organization in production. Production will no longer be directed by isolated manufacturers, independent of each other and ignorant of man's economic needs; that will be done by a certain public institution. A central committee of management, being able to survey the large field of social economy from a more elevated point of view, will regulate it for the benefit of the whole of society, will put the means of production into suitable hands, and above all will take care that there be constant harmony between production and consumption. Institutions already exist which have assumed as part of their functions a certain organization of economic labour, the banks.' We are still a long way from the fulfilment of Saint-Simon's forecast, but we are on the way towards it: Marxism, different from what Marx imagined, but different only in form.'[1]

A crushing 'refutation' of Marx, indeed, which retreats a step from Marx's precise, scientific analysis to Saint-Simon's guess-work, the guess-work of a genius, but guess-work all the same.

[1] *Grundriss der Sozialökonomik,* S. 146.

FURTHER READINGS

There exists a vast body of literature on imperialism. Below is a select bibliography. More comprehensive bibliographies can be found in some of the readings listed below. In the case of the classics, the references are to convenient later editions.

Classics

Bukharin, N.I., *Imperialism and the World Economy*, London: Merlin Press, 1972.

Hilferding, R., *Finance Capital*, English translation edited by Tom Bottomore, London: Routledge and Kegan Paul, 1981.

Hobson, J.A., *Imperialism: A Study*, London: Allen and Unwin, 1968.

Luxemburg, R., *The Accumulation of Capital*, London: Routledge and Keegan Paul, 1951.

Tarbuck, K., (ed.), *Imperialism and the Accumulation of Capital* London: Allen Lane, 1972. (Contains Rosa Luxemburg's *Anti-Kritik* and Nikolai Bukharin's critique of Luxemburg.)

Later Writings

Amin, S., *Unequal Development*, New York: Monthly Review Press, 1976.

———, *Imperialism and Unequal Development*, London, 1977.

———, G. Arrighi, et al., *Dynamics of Global Crisis*, New York: Monthly Review Press, 1982.

———, *Capitalism in the Age of Globalization*, Delhi: Madhyam Books, 1997.

Arrighi, G., *The Geometry of Imperialism*, London: Verso, 1983.

Bagchi, A.K., *The Political Economy of Underdevelopment*, Cambridge: Cambridge University Press, 1982.

Baker, D., G. Epstein and R. Pollin (eds.), *Globalization and Progressive Economic Policy*, Cambridge: Cambridge University Press, 1998.

Baran, P.A., *The Political Economy of Growth*, New York: Monthly Review Press, 1962.

———, and P.M. Sweezy, *Monopoly Capital*, New York: Monthly Review Press, 1966.

Brewer, A., *Marxist Theories of Imperialism: A Critical Survey*, London: Routledge & Kegan Paul, 1980.

Chomsky, N., *Profit Over People*, Delhi: Madhyam Books, 1999.

Emmanuel, A., *Unequal Exchange*, London: New Left Books, 1972.

Frank, A.G., *Capitalism and Underdevelopment in Latin America*, Harmondsworth: Penguin, 1975.

Halliday, J., and G. McCormack, *Japanese Imperialism Today*, Harmondsworth: Penguin, 1974

Hobsbawm, E.J., *Industry and Empire*, Harmondsworth: Penguin, 1969.

Horowitz, D., *From Yalta to Vietnam*, Harmondsworth: Penguin, 1967.

Kemp, Tom, *Theories of Imperialism*, London: Dobson Books, 1967.

Magdoff, H., *The Age of Imperialism*, New York: Monthly Review Press, 1969.

———, *Imperialism: From the Colonial Age to the Present*, New York: Monthly Review Press, 1978.

Monthly Review, 'Capitalism at the End of the Millennium', July–August 1999.

Owen, R., and B. Sutcliffe (eds.), *Studies in the Theory of Imperialism*, London: Longman, 1972.

Patnaik, P. (ed.), *Lenin and Imperialism*, Delhi: Orient Longman, 1986.

Patnaik, P., *Whatever Happened to Imperialism and Other Essays*, Delhi: Tulika, 1995.

———, *Accumulation and Stability Under Capitalism*, Oxford: Clarendon Press, 1997.

Pierre, J., *The Pillage of the Third World*, New York: Monthly Review Press, 1969.

Radice, H. (ed.), *International Firms and Modern Imperialism*, Harmondsworth: Penguin, 1975.

Rhodes, R.I., *Imperialism and Underdevelopment: A Reader*, New York: Monthly Review Press, 1970.

Varga, E., *Politico-Economic Problems of Capitalism*, Moscow: Progress Publishers, 1969.

———, and L. Mendelsohn, *New Data for V. I. Lenin's 'Imperialism, the Highest Stage of Capitalism'*, London: Lawrence and Wishart, 1939.

Warren, Bill, *Imperialism: Pioneer of Capitalism*, London: New Left Books, 1980.

INDEX

Karl Marx's classic work reissued in a beautifully bound hardcover set
from LeftWord Books.

Capital

Volumes I, II, III

Karl Marx

978-81-87496-94-6, pp. 768 + 564 + 960, hardcover

Volume I
A Critical Analysis of Capitalist Production
Translated from the third German edition by Samuel Moore and Edward Aveling and edited
by Frederick Engels
978-81-87496-95-3, pp. 768, HC

Volume II
A Critique of Political Economy
The Process of Circulation of Capital edited by Frederick Engels
978-81-87496-96-0, pp. 564, HC

Volume III
A Critique of Political Economy
The Process of Capitalist Production as a Whole edited by Frederick Engels
978-81-87496-97-7, pp. 960, HC

Special discounts available for Book Club Members. For details of Book Club Membership and
to order and pay online via a secure payment gateway, visit **www.leftword.com**. You can
also send cheques/drafts in favour of **LeftWord Books** to:

LeftWord Books, 12 Rajendra Prasad Road, New Delhi 110001 INDIA
www.leftword.com
leftword@gmail.com